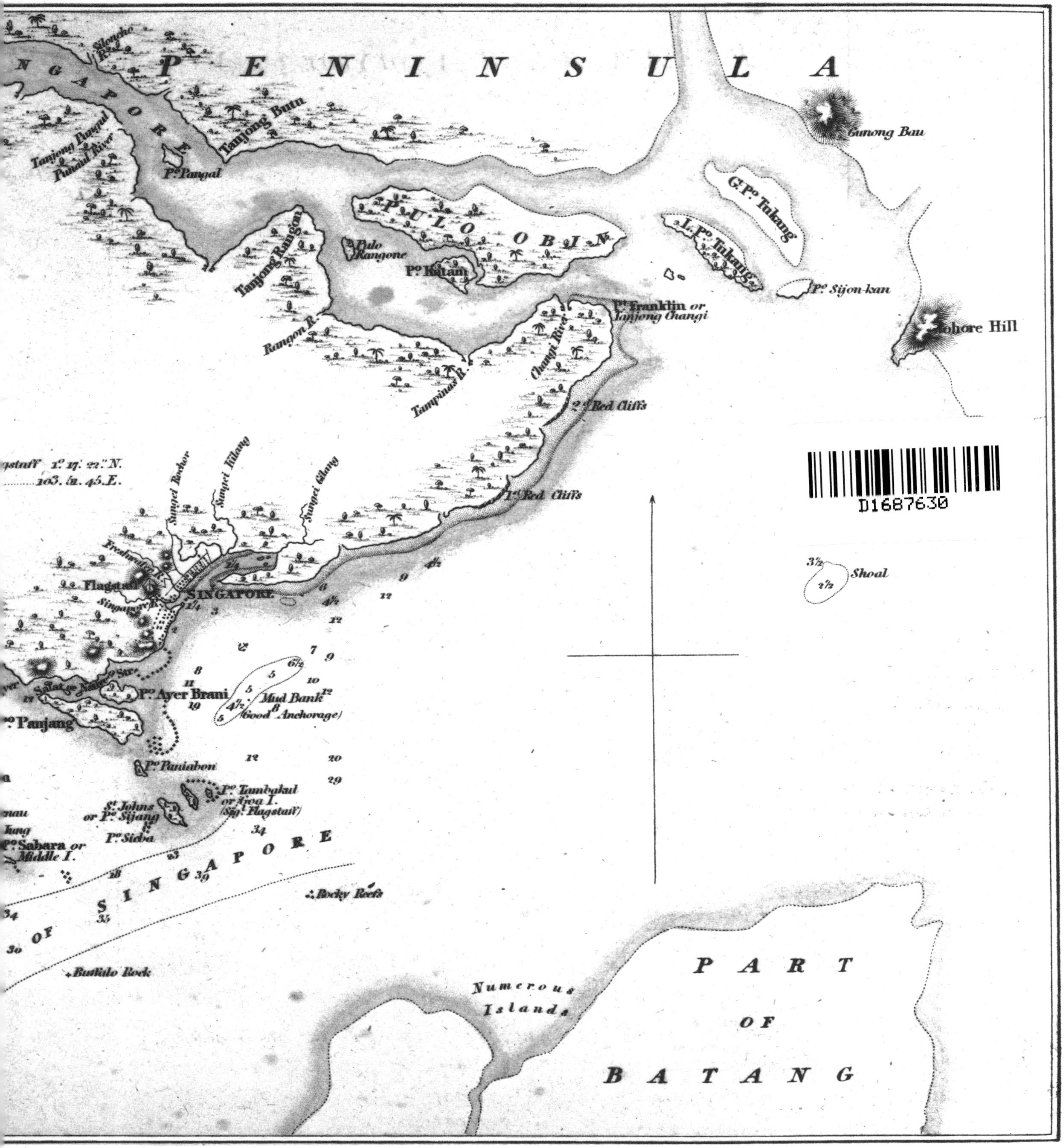

PENINSULA
NGAPORE
Silencho R.
Tanjong Butn
Tanjong Pungul
Punaul River
Pº Pangal
PULO OBIN
Pulo Rangone
Pº Katam
Tanjong Rangon
Rangon R.
Tampinus R.
Changi River
Gunong Bau
Gᵗ Pº Tukang
L. Pº Tukang
Pº Sijon-kan
Pᵗ Franklin or Tanjong Changi
Johore Hill
2ᵈ Red Cliffs
1ˢᵗ Red Cliffs
Flagstaff 1º 17' 22" N.
103. 51. 45. E.
Sungei Rochor
Sungei Kilong
Sungei Gilang
Freshwater R.
Flagstaff
Singapore R.
SINGAPORE
Shoal
Mud Bank (Good Anchorage)
Pº Ayer Brani
Pº Panjang
Pº Paniabon
Pº Tambakul or Goa I. (Sig. Flagstaff)
Sᵗ Johns or Pº Sijang
Pº Siba
Pº Sabara or Middle I.
STRAITS OF SINGAPORE
Rocky Reefs
Buffalo Rock
Numerous Islands
PART OF BATANG

Impressions of Singapore

Impressions

Geoffrey Dutton

# of Singapore

TIMES BOOKS International

Photographs by Harri Peccinotti

For Nan and Dean Hay, friends of mine and of Singapore

Many a green isle needs must be
In the deep wide sea of misery,
Or the mariner, worn and wan,
Never thus could voyage on.

PERCY BYSSHE SHELLEY.

Text © Geoffrey Dutton
Photographs by Harri Peccinotti
Editor: Gregory Vitiello
Art director & designer: Derek Birdsall
Production: Martin Lee
Typesetting by Balding & Mansell
Printed in Singapore by Tien Wah Press (Pte.) Ltd.

First published 1981 by
Times Books International
Time Centre, 1 New Industrial Road, Singapore 1953

All rights reserved. No part of this publication may be reproduced or transmitted, in any form or by any means, without permission from the original publisher

ISBN 9971 65 106 8

Preface

The Singapore 'miracle' has fascinated many people throughout the world. This extraordinary city-state, with its multi-ethnic and multi-national spirit, has shown what a mixture of peoples and races can achieve with the power and advantages they have when they work together. Mobil, itself a multi-national organization, especially appreciates this achievement.

With its particular commitment to Singapore, Mobil thought it would be interesting to have an outsider's impression of the 'miracle'. From the South we commissioned noted Australian writer, historian and poet, Geoffrey Dutton, to give his written impressions. From the North, we asked internationally renowned English photographer, Harri Peccinotti, to give his visual impressions. This book is the result.

We are particularly grateful for the introduction contributed by Professor Tommy Koh, Singapore's Permanent Representative to the United Nations.

We hope these 'impressions' will be appreciated and enjoyed by many Singaporeans and non-Singaporeans alike.

D.C. Dunn
Chairman, Mobil Oil Singapore Pte. Ltd.
January 1981

Acknowledgements

I would like to thank a number of people who helped me in several ways with this book.

First of all, of course, those from Mobil who commissioned the book and have been invaluable at every stage of its progress: Mr Y. Sugihara, who was Chairman of Mobil Oil Singapore during the genesis of this book and provided enthusiastic encouragement; the Board of Directors; Peter Wilkinson, and his wife Judy, Arun Mahizhnan and Christine Chan Wan Chiang, all of Mobil Singapore; and Captain David Sheehan, who organized our flight to Bencoolen in Sumatra.

The late Mrs. Lee Chin Koon, and her daughter-in-law Mrs. Pamela Lee Suan Yew, were particularly kind and generous of their time in telling me about the lives of the Straits Chinese.

William Lim Siew Wai and his wife Lina hospitably provided a venue for fascinating discussions about every aspect of life in Singapore, and a bookshop where I could find what was in print about Singapore.

Tay Kheng Soon and Dr. Chan Heng Chee gave me the benefit of a number of stimulating conversations.

Kirpal Singh, Chandran Nair and Robert Yeo were both hospitable and most informative about the state of literature in Singapore.

John Drysdale, Dennis Bloodworth and Ken and Ronnie Hillborne gave me access to some of the insights of their deep knowledge of Singapore.

K.C. Yuen, Director of the Singapore Tourist Promotion Board, was most helpful in a number of ways.

Finally, my wife and I, during our stay in Singapore, were most beautifully looked after by Mrs. Ah Fong.

It would be invidious, or in many cases impossible, to mention by name all those to whom I talked about Singapore, from those in the highest positions in government, administration and business, to those chance acquaintances in the streets, restaurants and shops of Singapore whose friendliness enables one to cross all barriers.

In writing this book I have had the great advantage of working once again, as in *Patterns of Australia*, with a team that manages to combine impeccable professionalism with unfailing wit and geniality. I refer to Harri Peccinotti who, with his assistant Genevieve Hamelet, took many hundreds of beautiful photographs of Singapore, from which the selection in this book was made; Greg Vitiello, Mobil Oil Corporation, editor of rare acumen; and Derek Birdsall, prince of designers.

Geoffrey Dutton

Foreword

The change in Singapore has been dramatic. It is a necessity of life in our crowded, dynamic country whose 2.4 million inhabitants occupy only 600 square kilometres of land. But while Singapore changes, we must work to retain its essential character. Modernity need not mean an end to our traditions or values. We must maintain a balance – a balance between old and new, and a balance in judging and appreciating Singapore as a social entity. For that reason "Impressions of Singapore" represents a meaningful contribution.

In this book, two non-Singaporean artists – an Australian writer and an English photographer – have recorded their impressions of our land and its people. They have been truthful and positive. They have called attention to Singapore's enduring needs: the need for greater community and national purpose, and a greater regard for our national past.

I wish to thank Mobil Singapore for sponsoring this book.

Ong Teng Cheong
Acting Minister for Culture
January 1981

Introduction

I have always felt the need for a good general book about Singapore. Such a book should consist of both pictures and text. The pictures should capture vivid images of the land and its people, in their many moods and faces. The text should give the vital statistics but it should not be confined to a recital of desiccated figures. Instead, it should give the readers a distillation of the events, forces and personalities which shaped the nation, a sense of the sound, colour, texture and rhythm of the society, an assessment of the nation's achievements and failures, an insight into what makes the place tick and an understanding of its dreams and nightmares.

It is not easy to produce a good book of this genre for it requires a balanced combination of extraordinary pictures and a brilliant text. Harri Peccinotti's photographs of Singapore are sensitive and lovely. Geoffrey Dutton's text is both interesting and insightful. Together they blend into an excellent general book on Singapore.

The Singapore story is worth telling and Geoffrey Dutton has told it well. It is a story about heroes – Stamford Raffles, whose vision led to the foundation of modern Singapore and Lee Kuan Yew, whose unique combination of political acumen and managerial skills, enabled him to fulfil Raffles' dream. It is a story of the triumph of reason over prejudice. Singapore is the confluence of three of Asia's principal peoples and cultures – i.e. the Chinese, Indian and Malay. They speak many tongues and worship many gods. But they have learnt to live together in one family and to practise tolerance.

It is the story of the triumph of optimism over pessimism. In the 1950's the British colonial government described Singapore's housing shortage as endemic and incurable. Today, two-thirds of the total population of Singapore live in public housing. In the 1950's and early 1960's the rate of unemployment in Singapore reached alarming proportions. Today, it is lower than the rate in most Western countries. In 1965, Singapore's per capita G.N.P. was US $500. Today, it is over US $3,000. The story of Singapore is a vindication of the human spirit. It is a reminder to us all that with intelligence, hard work and discipline most problems are capable of solution.

Geoffrey Dutton has praised the achievements of Singapore. He has also pointed out its shortcomings and failures. The rat race in Singapore starts at an early age and probably ranks among the worst in the world. The society is crassly materialistic. Eating, shopping and gambling are the only three 'performing arts' widely appreciated in Singapore. The frontiers of political and cultural freedom could also be extended.

No country, no society is without its shortcomings and problems. The same is naturally true of Singapore. But with Singapore's pulsating energy, its brains and its skills, one can be reasonably optimistic that it will tackle its problems in the educational and cultural fields as successfully as it has tackled those in the economic and other fields.

Professor Tommy T.B. Koh
Ambassador, Permanent Representative of Singapore to the United Nations, High Commissioner to Canada

January 1981, New York.

Moonlight over the City

Travellers' palm, Tanglin Road

Peacock, Jurong Bird Park

Bamboo, Bukit Timah Nature Reserve

Flora and Fauna, Botanical Gardens

Flamingoes feeding, Jurong Bird Park

Dawn, Peirce Reservoir

East Coast Shoreline

Bumboats, Singapore River

Sunrise

Sunrise

Rush hour, North Bridge Road

Rush hour, Paya Lebar

First impressions

Even when you fly into Singapore it is the harbour, and its hundreds of ships and boats, that dominates the scene. Thanks to many islands, and not being exposed to the surf of a rolling ocean, it is all open, and most of the ships ride out in the roads. Only the sampans and lighters hide like a myriad of beetles in the cleft of the rather absurd little Singapore river.

It is a wonderful approach, by air, especially from the south. There are so many islands, Raffles' Eastern Isles, covered with jungle, and if inhabited at all, only by people whose lives are discreetly a part of water and land, their presence never intrusive. You are in the tropics, just north of the Equator, and you come down over clouds the colour of crushed black grapes, over the islands of the tidal rivers so calm that the water seems to have just oozed over the land in a slow flood. Then suddenly there is Singapore, and the jet flies right along the waterfront, over the huge tankers and the little rusty coastal trading ships, and the brilliant buildings proclaim the presence of man and his works over the milky green water, while in the background the clusters of high-rise apartments are unexpectedly graceful and surrounded by green, like dancers holding still before an audience of trees.

There is a balance achieved already, for the little crowded island, nearly two and a half million people on little more than 600 square kilometres, came into existence, and exists now, only by favour of the sea. Singapore has no land in the sense of countryside, no crops or flocks or herds, no minerals, but it is the conductor through which the energies of lands all over the world flow. And the sea, conservator of its own energy, is the supreme conductor.

It is impossible for Singapore to live in isolation, since, unlike any other great port in the world, it is already physically isolated, having no hinterland. Nor, however prosperous it may be, can it afford the complacency of inherited wealth. All that it inherits is its geographic position and the skills, brains and energy of its people. It has to be dynamic or perish. It has no unexpected resources or fertile strength of its own; these must be supplied by human beings. In this, paradoxically enough, though it is an island and stays put, it is remarkably like a ship. It has to be doing something, otherwise it rusts away. It has to be charged with oil, kept serviced and clean, and be guided. It is a human invention, and exists only for commerce, for carrying cargoes or tourists, yet it is never without beauty, even mystery, and has a world of odd history behind its clear-cut exterior.

Stamford Raffles, who created modern Singapore, knew exactly what he was doing, even if the East India Company and the British Government did not. Though he hated the Dutch and wanted to secure for England the supremacy of trade in the Eastern waters, he was too great a man not to have a vision for his city; and like the most profound writer to know Singapore, Joseph Conrad, the East meant more to him than trade.

For Conrad, a ship also meant more than trade. Conrad was a young man, pulling and baling in an open boat for dear life from his burnt, sunken ship, when he saw the coast of Sumatra, and was brought thence to the safety of Singapore. It was his introduction to the East, which he never forgot: *This was the East of the ancient navigators, so old, so mysterious, resplendent and sombre, living and unchanged, full of danger and promise.*

When Conrad woke in the morning in his little boat made fast to the jetty, his dead-tired crew still sleeping, he saw *the men of the East — they were looking at me. The whole length of the jetty was full of people. I saw brown, bronze, yellow faces, their black eyes, the glitter, the colour of an Eastern crowd.* Those Eastern Isles had a powerful, physical magic, but it was brought alive by that extraordinary mixture of peoples.

And it was Raffles' fascination with the people of the East, and his mastery of the Malay language, that led him to Singapore. Raffles was Lieutenant-Governor of Bencoolen in Sumatra, none too young and none too well at 36, when he wrote on the last day of January 1819, *Here I am at Singapore, true to my word, and in the enjoyment of all the pleasure which a footing on such classic ground must inspire.* He had read the story of the destruction of the ancient 14th-century city Singapura, Lion City, or Temasek, in the *Malay Annals*, the Sejarah Melayu, when Singapura's ruler, Sultan Iskandar Shah, or Parameswara, was driven out, and founded the city of Malacca.

For Raffles' Malays and Conrad's 'Men of the East' there was of course no sense of living in 'the East.' The essence of Singapore's strength was that, although it may be 'the East' when viewed from London, it was at the heart of the compass on the ship riding at anchor in its harbour.

Singapore receives ships from all over the world, and it is in itself also the centre of South-East Asia, one of the richest and most populous areas on earth, whose inhabitants have, most encouragingly, come to realize what power and advantages they will have if they work together. The sea that connects them all deals very gently with Singapore. There are storms, of course, but the many islands protect the Straits of Singapore, and the water is so deep off shore that big ships can anchor and be peacefully unloaded by lighters.

The approach to Singapore by air is majestic, but no one has seen Singapore who has not spent several hours on the harbour, going between the ships and the islands and at the same time always aware of the huge presence of the city. There are so many ships, about 200 of them on the average, that it is hard to get the scale of them. A 250,000 tonne tanker in the far distance could be anything, but when it slowly comes closer it makes the cargo ships look like dinghies. And when you come right alongside it on the water it is a cliff-high island with a patch of rust the size of a house. So many of the ships are rusty, especially those registered in Liberia or Panama, although the bridges are painted white, so when the sun gets low it lights up bright bridges all over the harbour. Names, alas, are now mostly boringly utilitarian or somewhat absurd, *John F. Smith* or at best something like *Cherry Laju*, rather than the old names like *Flying Cloud* or *Lightning*. An elderly not-so-white liner turns out to be a pilgrim ship leaving shortly for Jeddah. The beautiful, spotless white ship tied up to the wharf is one of the Swedish cruise ships, buses waiting beside it to take aged passengers ashore to spend a pilgrim's savings in an afternoon. One of them has a *Straits Times* with a photo of customs officers standing around a haul of hundreds of bottles of whisky, cognac and liqueurs intercepted in a small boat coming in from the Philippines. Singapore's historical hospitality as a free port does not extend to smugglers or pirates, though both still exist.

Kelong

Harbour lights

On the one side there are ships at anchor; on the other the glittering, silver-white city buildings, all so new and so high, beyond the new sand of the reclaimed land and the new, instant trees growing past the pylons of the new freeway that will connect the city to the new airport at Changi. The pylons not yet joined to the track present a marvellously abstract sculpture, like the work of the German Herbert Hajek. Each leans outwards, glaring white, and between them in the distance is the straight plumb-line of the skyscrapers. The water is shining turquoise, degenerating to a polluted grey near Clifford Pier where the ferries and small boats cluster like sea-birds around a school of sardines. The freeway, where it is completed, already introduces an entirely new line, a curving one like the rim of the earth seen from a satellite, across the vertical buildings and the horizontal harbour. Out across the water, which is like milky jade here, a yellow oil pipe sleeps like a sea snake on the cloud-reflecting water, and those great clouds of the tropics lend a third rhythmic line, of towering curves and temporary opulence.

Between the big ships and the shore there is a constant traffic of sampans and lighters and barges, but even on holidays there is hardly a sound of a pleasure boat. In Singapore Harbour, you don't see the myriad yachts and power boats of, say, Sydney Harbour, for Singapore is more serious and more careful with its money.

The constant movement of barges and sampans, rather than pleasure boats, reflects the true nature of Singapore. A little tug goes past, towing a huge, high black barge, doubly black against the white skyline, where a Chinese steersman swings on a three metre tiller against a rudder three times the height of a man, rising out of the water in great stepped planks. The eyes, carved and painted on the bow, are part of the ancient rhythm of wood and water, steersman and tiller, but the practical and incongruous present always asserts itself in Singapore, in the car-tyre buffers along the side of the barge, and the shiny tin hut in the bows. On this barge the steersman has no shelter from the sun; but on three other barges with squared-off bows like junks and two masts that curve back their bare poles as if a gale of sails were on them, a vast awning of canvas billows over the steersman.

The sun demands this courtesy. The dominating presence over sea, ships and buildings is the sun beating back off the water, sometimes deceptively genial in the sea-breeze; but even when hidden by cloud or darkness it makes that constant tropical statement of heat. The other constant presence in Singapore and the tropics is of course humidity. On the harbour salty human sweat is like a homage to the sea, reminding one of the origins of life in the sea, and the fluid composition of the body.

On Singapore Harbour you are always conscious of three of the ancient elements, water, air and fire. But the fourth element, earth, is in steady if often invisible motion. Hundreds of barges and dredgers are busy dumping earth in the sea or moving it from the bottom to the shore. Perhaps the weirdest craft on the harbour are the giant dredgers, which in the bow look like a ship, with bridge and masts, while in the stern there is nothing but a colossal orange crane and a dredge with jaws the size of a truck that come up closed on several tonnes of harbour bottom, then let go into a waiting barge.

Raffles' map of Singapore Harbour, or the early paintings and engravings, reveal a coastline quite different from that which exists now. Where there was once water there are now some of the biggest buildings in the business section of Singapore, or high-rise apartments, playing fields, airports, warehouses. Hills and islands disappear, their rocks tumbled from trucks and barges into the retreating sea.

Hell, islands, says an old Harbour skipper, *they move them all over the bay!* Nearby, a green island with a yellow and white exposed headland shrinks into the sea as explosives shatter a cliff and bulldozers rattle rocks and soil into the barges. When the red-back barges, grey with rock, are towed into place, so low in the water they are almost sinking, a hidden lever is suddenly pulled and, as a cloud of dust rises, the barge shudders up empty out of the water.

Other islands are safe, preserved for industry or recreation. One has a temple on a hill and people swimming off its beaches. Another looks ready to sink into the sea under the weight of oil tanks and refinery towers, so that sometimes the leaping flame of the burning refinery gases seems like the exhaust pipe of some giant engine keeping the whole island afloat.

The container ships in the harbour always look odd when laden, so temporary, as if the whole batch of boxes would topple off if a few cables snapped. Joseph Conrad would have been hard put to find the romance of the sea in a container ship. Or in a giant liquid petroleum gas tanker, its white cupolas like cumulus clouds settled on the water. Next to it three tugs thrash the water as they push a 250,000 tonne tanker into the wharf for repairs. Beyond, a deep-laden cutter-rigged sailing-boat with red sails is gliding around the point of an island. And out in the bay a tiny little boat with an outboard motor is anchored, with a whole Chinese family fishing under a white canopy.

Sentosa Island, sheltering Keppel Harbour, is connected by a cable-car to the station on top of Mount Faber. Its original inhabitants, Malay fishermen, were removed so that it could be transformed into a tourist resort, but even with its golf course, its hotel, swimming lagoon, the Coralarium, gardens and camp site, it does not as yet make a convincing presence. It looks faintly irresponsible amidst all the serious activity of the harbour, and disorganized beside the cranes of the container wharf or the chimneys of refineries. Sentosa needs to be surrounded by a flurry of pleasure craft, of small sailing boats and catamarans. An island of unprogrammed personal enjoyment does not seem valid inside the network of the Singapore Port Authority, where the hundreds of ships are all there for a purpose, and the precision of airport controllers is needed to bring ships to the right wharf or anchorage.

All this harbour along the face of Singapore City is only part of the whole picture. Ships come in all around Singapore Island. At Jurong, the industrialized end of the island, there is a port and a marine base that handles and services thousands of ships and millions of tonnes of cargo a year. Sembawang Shipyard in the Straits of Johore, the old British Naval Base, is real enough, but its historical presence is forever washed with irony, with the surge of clichés that greeted the opening of the King George VI dry dock in 1938, of which the *Sydney Morning Herald's* selection is probably unsurpassed: *The Gibraltar of the East . . . the gateway to the Orient . . . the bastion of British might.* Then there is Serangoon Harbour, and

Sand and water

Gas and clouds

29

boats in inlets all around the island, and the sailing clubs near Changi. The other great ports of the world depend on rivers or bays for shelter; only Singapore is an island, with the sea all around it.

*   *   *

It is fitting that the founder of modern Singapore, Raffles, should have been born at sea, the son of a sea captain. Raffles, with his poverty-stricken youth and lack of education, would also have sympathized with the frequent economic crises and haphazard cultural development of Singapore's early days, before it achieved its present maturity.

C.E. Wurtzburg, author of the great biography *Raffles of the Eastern Isles*, quotes Admiral G.A. Ballard as saying that Raffles was *an English landsman with a range of maritime vision little inferior to that of Albuquerque*. Raffles was a great deal more humane and knowledgeable about the native peoples of the region than Alfonso D'Albuquerque, the conquerer of Malacca. Though Raffles masterminded Lord Minto's successful invasion of Java, he preferred to work through treaty and a sense of mutual benefit rather than exercises of war. Like Albuquerque, his maritime vision was not a simple one of great fleets, but a complex one involving ports and trading stations. Through his study of the Malay language and the extraordinary history of the region, he was able, on his arrival as Assistant Secretary of Penang in 1805, and his residence as Lord Minto's Agent in Malacca in 1810 and 1811, to see the whole region in perspective, from Java to Siam, from Borneo to India.

In the enchanting if not always factually correct memoirs of Munshi Abdullah, a member of Raffles' Malayan staff, there are some brilliant observations of Raffles' character and pursuits. *He was an earnest enquirer*, says Abdullah, *into past history and gave up nothing until he had probed it to the bottom . . . now, Mr. Raffles took great interest in looking into the origin of nations, and their manners and customs of olden times, examining what would elucidate the same. He was especially quick in the uptake of Malay with its variations. He delighted to use the proper idioms as the natives do . . . I also perceived that he hated the habit of the Dutch who lived in Malacca of running down the Malays and they detested him in return; so much so that they would not sit down beside him. But Mr. Raffles loved always to be on good terms with the Malays, the poorest could speak to him . . . and if my experience be not at fault, there was not his superior in this world in skill or largeness of heart.*

Today, there are over 200 million people in the Malayan archipelago: Malaysia; Sumatra, Java and the other Indonesian Islands; the Philippines; parts of Timor and New Guinea. The key to the complexity of kingdoms that formerly existed in these regions is the Malay language. Raffles, writing in a letter about the foundation of Singapore, said: *But for my Malay studies I should hardly have known such a place existed; not only the European but the Indian world was also ignorant of it.* This was a slight exaggeration, as both Dutch and English sea captains knew of it, as did the Indians and Chinese, but basically true enough. Through Malay, and his study of the Indian, Chinese, Portuguese and Dutch traders and invaders, Raffles could always see beyond the confines, often very provincial, of whichever settlement in which he was living. He also was touched, like Conrad, by the romance of the region. Who could not be by such names as The Golden Chersonese?

Raffles knew that the whole trading pattern of the region, bringing Arabs and Chinese and Indians to the peninsula, depended on the monsoons. The winds of empires, gold, spices, tin, ivory, monkeys, slaves, all converged on the Straits of Malacca, at the southern end of which lie the Straits of Singapore. Two thousand years ago trade between China and India went through these Straits. The Maharaja of Sri Vijaya controlled the Straits of Malacca from his capital of Palembang and his other main city in Kedah, north of the modern Penang.

Raffles could not have been more fortunate, or more prescient – for with him it was always determination and forethought rather than luck – in the siting of the three settlements where he held official positions, Penang, Malacca and Bencoolen. (His other position was as Lieutenant-Governor of Java, after Britain's successful invasion and dislodgement of the French in 1811.) We know from Lady Raffles' *Memoir* of her husband that Raffles had long had the ancient ruined city of Singapura in mind for the establishment of a British post.

Raffles was aboard the *Modeste* when the huge British invasion fleet of 57 transports carrying 11,000 soldiers, accompanied by frigates and sloops, sailed past Singapore Island. Among those watching the fleet was the ruler of Johore (and owner of Singapore), the Temenggong, Tunku Abdul Rahman. In a fine piece of historical insight, C.E. Wurtzburg writes: *he and his followers gazed on the passage of this great armada with amazement. No one in those parts could have seen such a display of sea-power before. And as the Temenggong watched wide eyed this long procession of ships, Raffles assuredly had his eyes fixed on the ancient site of the historic Singapore, of which he had read the tragic story in the* Malay Annals. *So the two men stared in each other's direction, each unconscious of the other and unaware of the chain of circumstances that eight years later was to link their destinies together.*

In Raffles' case the chain of circumstances went back further, to his fortunate appointment as Assistant Secretary at Penang in 1805. Penang, with its hills and forests and long beaches, is a much more beautiful island than Singapore, but it has neither the harbour nor the geographical advantages of Singapore. What it did have was a model for Raffles in its founder, Captain Francis Light (whose son William would become the founder of the city of Adelaide in South Australia). Francis Light was the Captain of a 'country ship' (a trading ship based in India) who as early as 1771 perceived that, to counter the Dutch monopoly, Britain urgently needed 'a convenient magazine for trade', and that Penang, off the coast of Kedah, was just the place. For 15 years Light tried to persuade the East India Company to establish a station at Penang or Junk Ceylon (now Salang) where he had his own headquarters. Those in control of the East India Company had the greatest difficulty in understanding the importance of anything east of India, and it was not until 12 August 1786 that Light finally hoisted the British flag at Penang and named it after the Prince of Wales (later George IV), whose birthday it was.

Raffles was to remember the extreme dilatoriness of the East India Company, *the invincible supineness of our ruler*, and to adopt his own ways around it. Raffles also learned from Light's example, for

Steersman and tiller

Container ship and crane

Light was a sailor who understood the winds and seas of the archipelago, a patriot who believed Britain must establish herself against the influence of the Dutch, a man of humanity and enthusiasm who realized the prime importance of speaking to the Malays in their own language. Light is well remembered in Penang; he should also be remembered in Singapore.

Bencoolen, where Raffles also was based, lies on the exposed western coast of Sumatra, across the mountains from Palembang amid its swampy inlets. Raffles' territory was a strip of land about 500 kilometres long running from Krui in the south to Inderapura to the north, not far from Padang. There are still tigers and gibbons in the mountainous jungle, from which Raffles, who was later to found the London Zoo, filled his house with a variety of animals and birds.

The fact that Raffles spent, on and off, six years as Lieutenant-Governor of Bencoolen often disguises the speed with which he pursued his main object, the establishment of Singapore. What actually happened was a forerunner, in its concentrated precision and planning, of Lee Kuan Yew's Singapore. Raffles arrived in Bencoolen in March 1817. He left for Calcutta in September 1818 to see Lord Hastings. On 2 December he left Calcutta with instructions and authority to secure for Britain a free passage through the Straits of Malacca by the only effectual means, that of *the establishment of a station beyond Malacca, such as may command the southern entrance of those Straits*. On 31 December Raffles arrived at Penang, where two survey ships, the *Investigator* and *Discovery*, had been ordered to await him.

On 12 December, waiting *off the Sand Heads* near Calcutta, he wrote an historic letter to Marsden, the historian of Sumatra. *We are now on our way to the Eastward, in the hope of doing something, but I much fear the Dutch have hardly left us an inch of ground to stand upon. My attention is principally turned to Johore, and you must not be surprised if my next letter to you is dated from the site of the ancient city of Singapoora.*

Raffles' suspicions were correct. The Dutch had already pre-empted an alternative site at nearby Rhio or Riau. But no other place could have been as suitable as Singapore for Raffles' purposes. When Raffles' squadron anchored on the afternoon of 28

January 1819 *off the intended port of Singapore, near a fine sandy beach,* there were less than 100 small houses and huts at the mouth of the river, one large house belonging to the chief of Singapore, the Temenggong, Tunku Abdul Rahman, and about 30 families of Orang Laut (sea gypsies) living on boats and ashore further up river. The island was low and covered with jungle, with one high point, Bukit Timah (Tin Hill) rising 177 metres above the sea. There were tigers and monkeys in the jungle; in fact the last Singapore tiger was seen as late as 1932.

There were constitutional problems over the kingship of Singapore, following the death of the last Sultan of Johore. Tunku Long Hussein, the legitimate heir, had been dispossessed by his uncle, the Rajah of Rhio, and his younger brother, the Rajah of Linga. Nothing could have suited Raffles better; dealing directly with Tunku Long enabled him to bypass the Dutch at Rhio. Tunku Long, a fat and frightened man, was brought to Singapore. No doubt he was partly reassured by the Temenggong, who had seen the great fleet of Lord Minto and knew the sea power of the English, and partly by Raffles himself.

Munshi Abdullah, although he did not arrive until four months later, gives a convincing and indeed unforgettable account of Raffles' reception of Tunku Long:

Mr. Raffles then began to speak, smiling with infinite charm and nodding his head in deference, his words sweet as a sea of honey. Not only the hearts of men but the very stones themselves would have melted on hearing his words, spoken in dulcet tones, gentle enough to banish every anxiety and suspicion which might linger still in the innermost recesses of the human mind . . . as men of a sudden see the full moon shining in all its lustre on the 14th day of the month, so was the honesty and sincerity of Mr. Raffles apparent to Tunku Long.

The result was that Tunku Long (now referred to as His Highness Sultan Muhammud Shah, Sultan of Johore), the Temenggong and Raffles, under the seal of the East India Company, signed a treaty on 6 February 1819. The modern state of Singapore was founded. Captain Crawfurd of the *Investigator* recorded that everyone then *repaired to the banquetting tent; after the Sultan was seated, the principal Malays sat down promiscuously with the English, and a few royal bumpers were quaffed off with three times three, and a degree of jollity and fun went forward.* The Sultan's contribution was a suggestion that all the Dutch in Rhio should forthwith be murdered. All the English, said Crawfurd, formed *a horrible and disgusting loathing of his person.* Raffles' honeyed words must have concealed a considerable exercise of will.

Raffles appointed the recently promoted Lieutenant-Colonel William Farquhar Resident of Singapore. Farquhar had been at Penang, waiting to return to Britain on retirement after 15 years as resident of Malacca before the Dutch took over in 1818, and he agreed to postpone his retirement and take on the Singapore job. He spoke fluent Malay and had married a Malaccan girl. Later, when Raffles and Farquhar fell out, Raffles considered that Farquhar's 'Malay connexion' afforded openings for *an undue combination of peculiar interests.*

Singapore was, amusingly enough in its present context, 'a dependency of the Government of Fort Marlborough', i.e. Bencoolen. An allowance was to be paid to the two Malay princes, and item 12 of Raffles' Proclamation modestly hid the policy that, from temporary improvisation, was to turn into the foundation of Singapore's prosperity: *It is not necessary at present to subject the trade of the port to any duties – it is yet inconsiderable; and it would be impolitic to incur the risk of obstructing its advancement by any measure of this nature.*

One of the most entertaining aspects of history in the years before the advent of modern communications was the frequent inability of the right hand of power to know what the left hand was doing. In 1819 in London both the Board of Control of the East India Company and the Foreign Office, not wanting to provoke trouble with the Dutch, were busy repudiating Raffles as a mere commercial representative with no political authority. The Marquis of Hastings, Governor of Bengal, was hypocritically writing to the Dutch on 26 June, *The occupation of Singapore has been to us a source of profound regret.* Meanwhile Raffles, having returned to Singapore from Bencoolen on 31 May, was, as he wrote to his wife, *most agreeably occupied in marking out the future town.* The tyranny of distance, in the Australian historian Geoffrey Blainey's memorable phrase, can also inspire a benevolent dictatorship. Singapore

Silhouettes of Singapore: (1)

Silhouettes of Singapore: (2)

would never have been founded if London or Calcutta had been able to call Raffles on the telephone.

The extraordinary early success of Singapore was based on the combination of its geographical position and its establishment as a free port, free of the punitive dues and regulations imposed by the Dutch at Java or Rhio. There was nothing threatening about it, then or now. Raffles' declaration in a letter, *Our object is not territory but Trade; a great commercial emporium*, could have been written by Lee Kuan Yew. The next half of Raffles' sentence, *And a fulcrum, whence we may extend our influence politically as circumstances may hereafter require*, might also have been approved of by Lee Kuan Yew.

Within two years there were 10,000 inhabitants, rich Chinese, merchants from Malacca, old friends of Farquhar; a Hokkien, Tan Tock Seng, a penniless vegetable hawker from Malacca, who was to become a millionaire; wealthy Arab traders from Palembang and Borneo, heirs to 1,000 years of trade; Armenian merchants from Brunei and the Philippines, the first, Aristarchus Moses, arriving in 1820; 500 Bugis, who arrived from Rhio and built their *kampong* on the Rochore river, ensuring Singapore of a rich trade with the Bugis, a Malay Muslim people from the Celebes and Macassar. The first building contractor, an Indian, Naraiana Pillai, came with Raffles in May 1819. Two Scots, Alexander Laurie Johnston and Alexander Guthrie, arrived in 1819 and 1820, and Guthrie's firm is still flourishing in Singapore. Singapore was multi-racial from its foundation.

Soon thereafter, between July 1821 and January 1822, three of Raffles' four children and several of his closest Bencoolen friends and associates died. Raffles and his wife were themselves desperately ill. On 29 January 1822 he wrote to his cousin: *For the last six months I have been so completely unnerved that I have scarcely written to any of my friends at home . . . our hearts are nearly broken, and our spirits sunk, I fear not to rise again – at least in this country.*

It was Singapore that restored him to life. Not long afterwards he was writing from there: *The coldest amd most disinterested could not quit Bencoolen and land in Singapore, without surprise and emotion. What, then, must have been my feelings, after the loss of almost everything that was dear to me on that ill fated coast? After all the risks and dangers to which this my almost only child had been exposed, to find it grown and advanced, beyond measure and even my warmest anticipations and expectations, in importance, wealth and interest – in every thing that can give it value and permanence?*

So, Singapore, Raffles' *almost only child*, received the full impetus of Raffles' reviving spirits, as he planned the streets and squares of a city of *beauty, regularity and cleanliness*, abolished slavery, prosecuted gambling, instituted training schemes to turn convicts into useful settlers but above all made plans for education. He founded the Singapore Institution, contributing (S)$2,000 himself, which was to be a centre of South-East Asian studies with teachers in the local languages, the field of study taking in not only South-East Asia but Australia and the Pacific, China and Japan. Alas, the Singapore Institution was not completed and fell into ruin, denied funds by the East India Company and ignored by the Singaporeans who were more interested in making money than in advanced education. It was not until 1835 that funds were raised to complete the building and organize the school, which was renamed Raffles Institution in 1868.

* * *

Although Singapore is a very small island, only 42 kilometres in length and $22\frac{1}{2}$ in breadth, it was many years before settlement went inland from the town, apart from a few plantations. All the activity took place on the seafront. It has never ceased. In contrast with Captain Franklin and Lieutenant Jackson's map and plan of Singapore, drawn in the 1820's, a modern map of Singapore shows a coastline bulging, squared off and straightforward, all at the expense of the sea. What the early map does not show is that Raffles had already started the process, filling in swamps to create the Boat Quay and levelling a hill to form the present Raffles Place. Raffles also started the long history of Singapore's town planning, evicting people and tearing down old houses to form new developments. Although well-off Europeans and Asians were expected to live and work side by side, Raffles set aside areas for Arabs and Indians, a Chinatown west of the river, and a Bugis *kampong* to the East beyond Kampong Glam, a 50 acre area reserved for the Sultan and his followers. The Padang and the Cricket Club of today are on the Open Square of Franklin and Jackson's map.

Almost every aspect of Singapore's future development is present in those first plans, in the years of forethought that led up to them, and in Raffles' own character. The newness of Singapore, albeit within the ancient walls that are still visible, is paralleled by the newness of the modern Republic of Singapore, and gives to both an excitement, a chance for daring and skill to make much of opportunities that can be lost in older, hidebound societies. There are remarkable parallels between Singapore's founder and its present Premier. The combination of moral fervour and respect for education and the sciences, the courage and ability for quick, ruthless and unconventional decisions, a passion for language, the instinct for a fluid society that at the same time needs wise guidance, the devotion to family, the lack of the easy-going vices, the insistence on cleanliness and order, perhaps the lack of humour, are all equally characteristic of Raffles and Lee Kuan Yew. On the other hand, Lee Kuan Yew learned early not to make some mistakes that Raffles did.

* * *

Amidst all the exuberant planning, Raffles committed the least admirable action of his life by turning on his old friend Farquhar, without whose guidance Singapore could never have developed as swiftly and successfully as it did. Communications were so bad that months went by without Singapore hearing from Bencoolen; once Farquhar had to wait 11 months for a reply to a letter to Raffles. Farquhar had gone against Raffles' instructions, particularly in allowing the Sultan and Temenggong too many privileges, and in re-introducing gambling and cockfighting, and there were various other differences between the two men; perhaps Farquhar's worst mistake was announcing in 1820 that he was going to retire and then refusing to allow the successor appointed by Raffles to take over. Raffles' dismissal and humiliation of Farquhar was unforgivable. Farquhar must have been as pleased as Raffles was mortified by the tremendous farewell reception given him by the townspeople.

Highway to Changi Airport

Cable car to Sentosa

Raffles' back-breaking tragedies of 1821 and 1822 may explain, if not pardon, his treatment of Farquhar. It is much harder to explain his cruelty and explosive lack of sensitivity — one might almost add vulgarity — toward a Malay, Sayid Yasin. This man had been imprisoned for debt by Farquhar, despite the fact that Sayid was a man of rank. In March 1823 Sayid asked permission to see Farquhar, then pulled out a knife and killed a police *peon* and stabbed Farquhar before being cut down by Farquhar's *peons*. Raffles refused to hand the body over to the Sultan, and instead sent it round the town on a bullock cart to the sound of a gong, then hung it in a specially made iron cage for two weeks at Telok Ayer Point. In the account of C.B. Buckley, *The body was then buried at Tanjong Paggar, (which) . . . became a place of pilgrimage, and Syed Yassim was considered a great saint, because the holy Sayed had only killed a Fakir (the Hindoo) and wounded a Nazarene (Colonel Farquhar).*

Raffles may have wanted to warn anyone with ideas of running amok that the authority of the King of England would not stand such nonsense, but all he did was to stir up racial animosity. This alarmed the Europeans and Chinese, who were almost without police or military protection, and could easily have been wiped out by the Malays. The episode is symbolic of the violence that has always existed under the orderly surface of Singapore.

Raffles' behaviour might be explained by the fact that he was suffering appalling agony from what was probably a brain tumour, and had recently written to his old friend the Duchess of Somerset that: *I have had another attack in my head, which nearly proved fatal.*

The sea brought Raffles and the sea took him away, although the three visits and the few months he spent in Singapore determined its destiny. Singapore was the one place that neither disappointed him in itself nor unleashed any of the malevolence of fate on him as Bencoolen did. The sea itself was the setting for his final tragedy.

Raffles and his family, with all his goods and collections, valued at £25,000 but uninsured because he was based in Bencoolen, embarked on the *Fame* on 2 February 1823 for England. In the evening of the first day the steward went down with a candle to draw some brandy from a cask below. There was a flash, and in a minute the ship was ablaze and only by a miracle did the 41 souls aboard escape in the boats.

What Raffles lost is best told in his own words. *The loss I have to regret, beyond all, is my papers and drawings – all my notes and observations, with memoirs and collections, sufficient for a full and ample history, not only of Sumatra, but of Borneo, and almost every other Island of note in these Seas; – my intended account of the establishment of Singapore – the history of my own administrations; – Eastern grammars, dictionaries, and vocabularies; – and last, not least, a grand map of Sumatra, on which I have been employed since my arrival here, and on which, for the last six months, I have bestowed almost my whole undivided attention. This however, was not all; – all my collections of natural history – all my splendid collection of drawings, upwards of 2000 in number – with all the valuable papers and notes of my friends, Arnold and Jack; – there was scarce an unknown bird, beast, fish, or an interesting plant, which we had not on board; a living tapir, a new species of tiger, splendid pheasants, etc., domesticated for the voyage, we were, in short, in this respect, a perfect Noah's Ark.*

All, all has perished; but, thank God, our lives have been spared, and we do not repine.

When Raffles told Munshi Abdullah that he was leaving Singapore for England, Abdullah said, *My heart palpitated and my spirit was gone . . . I felt as if I had lost Father and Mother – such was my condition that my eyes were bathed in tears. When he perceived this his face became flushed and wiping his tears with his handkerchief he told me not to be disheartened for if he lived he intended to return to Singapore.*

Raffles did not live long enough, although he had time to found the Zoological Society of London. He was in ill health in London when the East India Company finally wrote in April a letter to say how they appreciated his services, especially in Java, and how much the country was indebted to him for securing to it the Settlement of Singapore. On the same day they sent him a bill demanding immediate repayment of £22,272 which they alleged he owed them, the sum in question being in no way a dishonourable debt but arrived at over 10 years by quibbles over his salaries and commissions in Java and at Bencoolen. This came a few weeks after the news that Thomas McQuoid's business house in Batavia had failed, and with it was lost the £16,000 Raffles had instructed them to remit to London.

On 5 July Raffles died of apoplexy. He was 45 years old.

He never returned to Singapore to keep his promise to Munshi Abdullah, who in turn wrote Raffles' best epitaph as a man. *There are many great men besides him, clever, rich and handsome, but in good disposition, amiability and gracefulness, Mr. Raffles had not his equal, and were I to die and live again such a man I could never meet again, my love of him is so great.*

His best epitaph as *a man of maritime vision* and a scholar of the *lingua franca* of South-East Asia, is Singapore, the city that unites the peoples amongst whom he spent his working life.

Water cargo

Land cargo

Community

Singapore, the happiest home of the technological and economic miracle, sometimes is in danger of acting as if it never had a past, or, if it did have one, that the evidence of it is rather grubby and shameful. Raffles' dream of the future is more than realized; what is being lost is his equally powerful vision of the cultures of the whole region, and an education which will respect the past as much as it acknowledges the hunger for the future.

Two of the most encouraging pronouncements from Singapore's leaders acknowledging the claims of the past have come, as recently as mid-1980, from Trade and Industry Minister Goh Chok Tong and Singapore Tourist Promotion Board Director K.C. Yuen. Mr. Yuen expresses well what both of them were saying on different occasions: *We have to make a concerted effort to preserve parts of Chinatown, not just one or two streets but the full city block, not just the building but the city life-style, e.g. Arab Street, Serangoon Road, and the Muslim quarters.* He added that this is not only for the sake of the tourists but also for future generations of Singaporeans who need to know what life was like for their forefathers in the early 1900's

Mr. Yuen has looked at the problem with the wide view that is necessary. He has not just talked about Chinatown, but about Arab Street, Serangoon Road and the Muslim quarters, recognizing that Singapore has always been multi-racial. Secondly, he has not made the mistake of wanting to preserve the past just for tourists. It is the Singaporeans themselves who deserve to be able to keep contact with their own history. Mr. Yuen might also have mentioned some of the more splendid old Chinese-Singapore houses that still survive, with their multiple reception rooms and inner courtyards open to the sky, their carved facades and balustrades of porcelain. Looking at such a house, under threat of demolition, with its old Baba (Straits Chinese) furniture still intact, one may be forgiven for speculating that in 10 years' time Singapore will be having a conservation campaign, but there will be nothing left to conserve.

Raffles envisaged from the beginning the predominant position of the Chinese in Singapore, and how from *the peculiar attraction of the place for that industrious race it may be presumed that they will always form by far the largest portion in the community.* It was a remarkably prophetic statement.

He knew what a complex people the Chinese are, and he gave instructions that in Chinatown west of the river, the people of different provinces should be kept separate, *under the immediate control of their own chiefs,* and that *the concentration of the different descriptions of artificers such as blacksmiths, carpenters, etc. in particular quarters should also be attended to.*

The Chinese came to Singapore from the sea, but they are not as close to the sea as they used to be, owing to the filling in of the harbour and the establishment of the main business section in the town between Chinatown and the sea. This makes even more abrupt the contrast between the glittering skyscrapers, sleek and unearthly as parts of machines, and the tiled roofs and intimate windows, sprouting with washing poles, of the shop houses below. It is the difference between aluminium and painted wood, ferro concrete and crumbling plaster.

And, of course, the contrast is not only with Chinatown. An intense and highly coloured life of infinite variety is concentrated in the traders of Arab Street, where in front of one shop is cheap costume jewellery; at the back, precious stones; and in another shop there are cotton dress lengths downstairs and gold brocaded silk saris upstairs. The same variety extends to the illusionist nightlife of Bugis Street; the cornucopia of a Hindu Temple; the austerity of a Mosque; and the people themselves, eager Indians, discreet Arabs, unhurried Malays.

Chinatown with its markets and trades and temples has the diversity and untidiness of history. Though thousands of tourists go there it is not 'a tourist attraction', an animated sideshow like Disneyland. It still exists primarily and adequately for the Chinese and their customers, and if it is destroyed in the name of the anonymous future, Singapore will be the poorer. What will be lost is the vibrancy of an authentic, historic way of life, the colour and ornament of small architecture, the intimacy of family lives based on what goes on downstairs or out in the street.

The early morning is the best time to see Chinatown, beginning with breakfast. The Chinese eat out at all hours and at all sorts of places. A guide like Mr. Lim Kim Guan is a great asset, as no foreigner would know the intricacies of life in Chinatown.

Mr. Lim recommends beginning with breakfast. At 8 a.m. the little restaurant is already crowded with men and women, its zinc-topped tables each with a gas-bottle underneath and a kettle singing on the burner in the middle of the table. The waiter brings a little pottery teapot and tiny cups and chrysanthemum tea in a new box. The pork ribs have been stewing in a delicious soup for 12 hours and they are as tender as they are tasty. Together with the rice are doughnuts. One of the attractions of Chinatown is that whatever you eat you can also see for sale or being made. In the doughnut shop there are three women with flashing hands, rolling, flattening, cutting, pulling, so the dough takes on its own life in their hands, elastic and then taut as a living thing; watching, one flinches as the doughnuts are dropped in the boiling oil, however briefly. Yet another woman ties the fresh doughnuts into bundles, wrapped in little squares of white paper, much nicer eaten fresh than at the restaurant.

One mystery about the Chinese is that they love to eat, at all hours, yet few of them run to fat. It is always a shock to fly from a Chinese society to a Western country, whether America, Australia, or in Europe, and see how fat and flabby people look after the trim Chinese, and how they wobble and slouch along compared to the Chinese who hold themselves straight and move firmly.

Food is what first strikes anyone in Chinatown streets, most of it brought from under or over the sea, as Singapore grows very little of its own food. Fresh fish swim in tanks, or lie in silvery ranks waiting to be seized by the fishmonger who cuts the head off, then slices them into cutlets with flashing strokes of a cleaver driven through the flesh and bone by a mallet which is simply a buffalo's horn. In a nest of smoked oysters, sausages, prawns, shrimps and dried squid a wrinkled woman of 90 with fingers quick as a girl of 19 sorts and peels shrimps. One is struck again by the speed with which the Chinese do anything, from making doughnuts to chopping meat or fish, from carving wood to making a suit of clothes, and from counting money to making money.

Chinese still life: (1)

Chinese still life: (2)

At a tortoise stall the creatures are alive, of all sizes, except for one about a foot across that has just been chopped into four and cleansed of its entrails. In the midst of its hollow chest, between its outstretched hands and feet, the heart is still beating. *See*, says Mr. Lim, pointing to it. *Soup and meat very good for ulcers. Best cure for ulcers, five or six live white mice only two or three hours after they are born, swallowed whole.*

To the side of another stall clustered thick with live, pinioned crabs, prawns and whiskery catfish, is an iguana from Sumatra, hands and feet tied behind his back with pink string. In his crumpled suit of spotted khaki skin, at the bottom of a bleached tub, he seems quite dead, but then a lidded eye opens and closes. He is alive, waiting to be boiled, and his flesh and the soup it makes will be good for asthma.

At the next stall there are big frogs in wire cages, their thighs as fat as pigeons'. Enormous brown fowls, the size of turkeys, are tethered by string. Suddenly a man grabs one, nicks its throat and runs the blood into a bowl, plunges the body into boiling water, then throws it into the plucking machine, whence it emerges clean, the head and comb somehow making it appear even more naked. Beside the stall there is a row of smoked ducks, a waxy, lustrous sheen to their skin and a faint leer on their stiffly bent heads.

Across the street there are two squirrels in football-shaped cages, seeming to treadle away quite cheerfully when Mr. Lim gives the cage a twirl. Further along there is a red metal cage containing a sleepy python which wakens rather unwillingly and opens and closes its jaws.

Then, of course, there are the vegetables and herbs, great heaps of greens, spinach, lettuce, horseradish. Two old ladies sit on the pavement peeling bean sprouts with a flick of their thumbs, and ranging them in two piles of sprouts and peel. The most delicious and pungent smells come from the herbs, that multitudinous Chinese garden of cures; amongst things dried and twisted, curled and antlered, are lotus buds in their classic purity, useful, as Mr. Lim engagingly puts it, *for asthma and for decoration.*

The street level of the shop-houses offers every activity known to man with the possible exception of nuclear physics. There are shoemakers' stalls bright with clogs, and cavernous dark rooms selling charcoal. In another shop a man is blending soya sauces, filling a tin dipper from a row of vats along the wall and mixing them to his taste. Across the front of the shop there is a row of big blue empty pottery jars, stained at the mouth with red chili sauce.

In another house there is a young man making the pastry for wrapping spring rolls. With extraordinary skill he spins the lump of raw paste on his right hand as he sits in front of a charcoal stove with its two polished hot plates glowing, and then brings it down on to the plate. Depending on how hard he pushes, he makes either a small pancake or a big one. In his left hand he holds a flat metal implement like a paint scraper, and as he presses the paste to the right-hand plate he is already flipping the cooked pancake off the left-hand plate on to the pile appropriate to its size. He lands each pancake exactly in place and each pile is exactly the same diameter. Suddenly he gets up, walks away and has a cup of tea. He certainly needs something to make up for the pressure of that work.

Mr. Lim points to a house with closed doors. *An opium den. The old people there are all addicts. When I was a boy all the streets were opium dens. My father would be here and sometimes my mother would go and fetch him home.* Another street was all for gambling. In another street Mr. Lim points and says delicately, *Those two houses, face each other, Tea Houses of August Moon.*

Mr. Lim is a Hokkien and his quarter is rather quieter and more open, with some trees and plants in the walls and a garden or two. There is also a haunted house where the victims of a Japanese massacre were thrown during the war. No one will live there or walk by it at night. Not far away a woodcarver is finishing a two-foot-high statue of Buddha, the pale wood curving off his chisel, and next to him his assistant is sandpapering a row of identical arms. Another assistant, a woman, is painting and gilding, while the finished works light up the street in rows in the window, and in the shadows of a high shelf, a tiger holds its tail high.

In another quarter there is Sago Lane, and Mr. Lim stops and says, *This is the Morgue. Someone died this morning.* It is a deathhouse, where old people are taken to die upstairs and then their bodies are brought down to be laid out. The steep narrow wooden stairs have treads so worn they are like bullock-yokes. *Those lanterns hanging there say he was 75*, continues Mr. Lim. *Come in and we will look at him.* Behind a dull blue wooden screen the corpse is laid out, a little old man, his face and most of his body covered with crisp paper painted with black characters, only his hands visible, and his feet in white socks and black slippers. *He is dressed like a Mandarin*, says Mr. Lim. He has a little round hat with a red button and his blue jacket hangs over one hand which lies extended over the edge of the table, and holds a fan. The other hand holds a white handkerchief. Beside him are gifts for the journey: two oranges, two round pink cakes, a bottle of stout and a bottle of soya sauce. Incense burns in a jar. No one else is there.

Across the street is the coffin maker. The old man's coffin is a simple one of stained pine with metal ornaments, as he is to be cremated. *Cheap*, says Mr. Lim, *only $400. Now those coffins*, he points to huge boxes of solid red teak with strange triple curving ends, *they are for burying — $2,000 each. Fourteen men to carry them.* Indeed, it is only just possible to lift one end of the enormous lid. Next door there is a shop that makes funeral offerings to be burnt, in paper, everything from fruit to motorcars.

Upstairs a birdcage hangs in the sun, there are faces at the windows, and a mirror outside to keep the evil spirits away and to guide straying husbands home. Half of the street is shaded by washing thrust out on poles from the windows to dry.

Whereas Christian churches make one conscious of death, Chinese temples are bustling with life, both in the businesslike worshippers and in the painted and gilded carvings and gold and red hangings. Although the faces of the women burning incense in front of a shrine are rapt in spiritual contemplation, there is also a boisterous amount of noise, and a sense of involvement, a waving of incense sticks to attract the deity's attention. In front of one shrine a woman is lighting a bundle of paper. *She is burning money*, says Mr. Lim. There is room for the devil, especially in two devil shrines, the devils wrapped in coarse hessian-like cloth, strings of coins around their necks, their faces dissolving away in a glistening

Hot chilies

Dried seafood

brown substance melting from their foreheads and the stumps of their noses down the front of their robes. *Opium*, says Mr. Lim.

The pragmatic Chinese view of life is present in the restaurant and the shop for incense and other things on the side of the temple, and in the fact (astonishing to those of other faiths) that the temple is privately owned. The proprietor, who inherited the business from his grandfather, is a cheerful fellow, like any good businessman concerned with the welfare of his customers, prepared to shake hands and be polite but not to linger too long in conversation.

Further down the street, outside a crowded restaurant, several men are eating, squatting on high stools, their knees level with their chins. *You know why they squat?* says Mr. Lim. *Because if you sit you close your bottom and then you can't eat so much. When you squat you open your bottom, and you eat more.*

And there are the great buildings, looking down, in more ways than one, on Chinatown, where the computers are blinking with never a stick of incense burned before them, gods though they be; and money slides in and out of safes behind bars, instead of being changed in the street, and six rows of cars sweep down the street between buildings as glass doors sigh open on the instructions of electric eyes. From Shenton Way to Sago Lane is a lot further than from Bencoolen to Singapore, but Raffles would no doubt happily make the journey, as he would be overjoyed to see those hundreds of ships in the harbour. No doubt, also, he would not flinch to see the bulldozers biting off great chunks of Chinatown, for his main consideration was always the long-term interests of Singapore, and how land and resources could be best utilised in the scientific planning of the city. He took the widest view. After all, he was just as emphatic that Singapore should have a Botanic Garden.

Nevertheless, the destruction of Chinatown diminishes Singapore.

As Hindu, Muslim and Christian cultures are all in evidence within walking distance of Chinatown, so the greatest Chinese festival, Chinese New Year, spills over into the lives of the other races that make up the Republic of Singapore.

On Chinese New Year flying trucks covered with New Year's

messages, and men beating drums and clashing cymbals and singing, have precedence on the roads, day after day for a week.

The Hok Kiaw Athletic Club surge up in their two trucks in front of the Shangri-La Hotel. The main drumbeater stands in a painted and decorated trailer, banners flying, by a huge drum stretched across a barrel big enough to hold enough beer for one whole night of Chinese New Year. Alongside him on the road the gong-player bounces on his sturdy legs, and a row of skinny cymbal-players clang and crash furiously in the hot sun. The drummer belts out an electrifying rhythm, so subtle in its variations, and he never tires, unlike the cymbal-players, who after a while are relieved between clashes and go off for a cool drink. In a corner of the drummer's trailer is a selection of food and a couple of large lettuces.

Now the enchanting spring-toed lions are dancing, one red and white, one red and yellow, each quite different in character from the other, their mouths opening and shutting, their eyelids fluttering, tails swishing, so gentle and genial, while the drummer is the fierce one, thrashing the rest of his percussion team on to new frenzies. A pair of monkeys – it is the Year of the Monkey – arrive and play with the lions, who show off by balancing on a little red table, and scratching their ears with fat paws.

Then there is an entire change in rhythm, as the lions are led away and two sweating men emerge from each of them. They were hairy Northern lions, and now two black and white striped lions from the South, with shorter coats – much more wicked fellows – come forward and begin to dance. Suddenly with another change in rhythm again, an irresistible syncopation, a jaunty gentleman masked in a huge glistening pink head, wearing a grey dustcoat and yellow trousers, steps out spryly to the rhythm and sets out tubs of cumquats, dusting them carefully, and several pots, and tea and food.

Then the lions, up to no good, dance around the pots, gobble up the food, and daringly balance on the pots, until one of them begins to hang his huge face low and droop his tail, and suddenly he sicks up a mound of lettuce leaves. Out comes the old pink tonsured gentleman and away go the lions and soon the trucks themselves are leaving, full of young men in yellow and red shirts, the cymbals still clashing.

It has all been free of charge. Maybe the hotel pays them something, but there is no doubt that the Hok Kiaw Athletic Club does it for fun.

So does all the astonishing mixture of old and young, Chinese, Indian and Malay, who take part in a Chingay Procession during the New Year celebrations. The word *Chingay* refers to a Chinese-style decorated float, and a number of these take part in the procession that also includes musicians, dancers, dragons and lions, stilt-walkers and huge flags which are rolled and whipped and spread on huge poles by men with chests like bears. The original idea of a Chingay Procession was to please the Chinese gods, but when the Government-backed People's Association and the Singapore National Pugilistic Federation sponsored the first modern Chingay Procession in 1973 the religious element was played down and the Chinese inspiration balanced, as befits a multi-racial society, with floats and groups from all the other races of Singapore.

Lee's earnest puritan Government encourages the Chingay for its benefits to the people. A little jollity and colour and festivity is good for them. To quote from the official programme: *The Procession is strongly diversified in its cultural forms and a contemporary element has been introduced. It is also colourful and impressive with its 2,000 participants and is to be enjoyed as a family outing. Although the spirit of competition motivating the sponsors of the Chingays of old is not encouraged, emphasis, nevertheless, is placed on the quality of the items presented.*

Going back three-quarters of a century, it is amusing to note the change of emphasis. Lee's spiritual and cultural ancestors, the serious Chinese of the early 20th century, who believed in education, order, dignity and respect, did not at all approve of the Chingay. In 1906, with the support of Dr. Lim Boon Keng and other Chinese leaders, Mr. Ong Hwee Ghee denounced the Chingay Procession at a meeting at the Hokkien temple.

Ignorant people, he said, *have the vulgar notion that worshipping the gods will bring good luck and sacrifices will avert calamities. To make matters worse, busy-bodies add to the folly of the ignorant by introducing*

Eggs on the move

Clogs in the making

prancing lions and paper dragons – in fact, the chingay procession – in order to please the gods. Now, even in China, such processions are prohibited by law, although when the country is enjoying peace and prosperity the Mandarins do not interfere . . . as for respecting the gods, reverence, accompanied with the burning of incense, is enough. What need is there to belabour the people and waste money in order to compete in the vulgar show in which unfortunate women are hired, and dressed up in gorgeous style and paraded through the streets to be seen of all nations. This sort of show I consider to be an insult to the gods, and I tell you that if the gods have any sense of honour, you must be thankful that they do not curse you for thinking them capable of enjoying such rubbish.

The gods are not much in the minds of those who watch the Chingay today. Grandstands are erected at the corners of Avenue 4 and Avenue 11 alongside the high-rise windows and balconies of Ang Mo Kio New Town, where at 8.30 in the morning the people are already crowding to watch the procession assembling, while the grandstands, mercifully shaded by cloud, are already almost full. At 8.45 at some mysterious signal there is a rush of people, especially children, to take up the vacant spaces remaining in the grandstand. It is interesting to see how the orderly Singaporeans behave on the grandstand as the procession begins and the clouds clear away and the morning grows hotter and hotter. First they all sit. Then children especially begin to stand to get a better view. Soon everyone is not only standing up but is standing on the seats. It is not so orderly after all. But when a European woman asks a group of Chinese children to move apart so she can take some photos, they all politely do as they are asked. The good manners of Singaporeans of all types and ages must never cease to amaze the citizens of ruder countries.

The Chingay Procession is one of the most pungent symbols of contemporary Singapore. The national identity is not just the four-footed lions and the 14-footed dragons. There is Bridal Joy, a Chinese wedding of big-headed dolls; Valli Thirumanam, a wooing of Indian gods; Mela Dharamveers, turbanned Sikhs dancing; Hanuman, the Monkey God from the *Ramayana*; the Ahmad Ibrahim Secondary School Band. The weird essence of Singapore is in the noises this crazy caterpillar makes as it wriggles down Street 11 into Avenue 3. The People's Association Choir, Dance Company and Singing Troupe are weaving around in the sun in Western and Chinese garb giving voice to *Singing in the Rain*. A band plays American marches, and then a collection of anonymous children caper around the television personalities in *Telefun on Parade*. This cultural event is exceeded in awfulness by another lot of children acting out nursery rhymes, four-and-twenty blackbirds emerging from the pie, boys and girls coming out to play to the familiar tune of what the announcer says is an old Chinese melody.

Poor James Barrie! If he could see Peter Pan at the Chingay! For somehow or another Peter Pan seems to have been through Disneyland and out the other side as he searches for the Henny Penny tribe, pursued by Red Indians, to an all-American song. Another ancient favourite lurches into a strange new life as the Vigilante Corps comes to town as a circus with Dr. Doolittle and his animal friends; but it is a selection of animals that never appeared in the books.

The most amazing sight and sound of all must surely be the Singapore Girl Pipers, Chinese, Indian and Malay girls in black velvet jackets, red shirts and unidentifiable tartan skirts, and long boots, playing tunes on the bagpipes.

Sometimes the Singapore National Identity seems like a meal where everyone simultaneously eats noodles, curry, hamburgers, Irish stew and Scots porridge.

Another good occasion to see the Singapore Identity in action is to be amongst 2,000 paying guests at the Neptune Restaurant, seated at tables around a stage, upstairs and downstairs. The occasion is a Singapore National Co-operative Union's fund-raising dinner for a Community Home for the Aged. It is interesting that such a project is necessary in socialist Singapore. The reasons are given in one of the many messages printed in the evening's programme, especially that of a fraternal one from the President of the Co-operative Union of Malaysia. He says, *Modernisation and development necessarily bring about social changes and social problems. Some of our Asian concepts and ways of life are affected by the rapid industrialisation and modernisation. For instance, it was a common practice for many Asian families to live together in their ancestral homes wherein the older and weaker members of the family were looked after by the younger members of the families. Today the modern conditions of living and environment make it impossible to continue such a practice. Consequently, changes are inevitable. Therefore, alternatives have to be found to cater for the social needs of the people who are least able to fend for themselves.* (This is a message which those who run the Housing Development Board and the high-rise new towns have received; they are making special efforts to allot nearby flats in the same building to those families who wish to keep grandparents and children close together. Even so, there are a lot of old people still uncared for.)

One never ceases to be astounded at the cheerful efficiency of the Chinese. In most countries a dinner for 2,000 is a culinary disaster served half-cold by grumpy waitresses and waiters, with never enough to drink. Not so at the Neptune, where the food is hot, varied and remarkably good, and the drink supply copious, all delivered by waitresses who seem to be thoroughly entertained by the whole gathering.

It is interesting also that the Singaporeans, once again seeming so orderly, don't quite turn out that way, as on the grandstand at the Chingay. They pay moderate attention to the Chairman of the Singapore National Co-operative Union who gives the opening address. But the Guest of Honour, the Minister of State for Defence, is soon denied the respect due either to a Minister or to Defence. He reads a long and rather surprising speech, the sort of address you might hear at a Seminar on 'The Phasing Out of the Co-operative Movement', the gist of which is that co-operative movements are completely out of date in modern Singapore, and although of course he is very happy if everyone wants to support a Home for the Aged, that sort of thing is much better taken care of by the Government. Already half-way through his speech most of the 2,000 guests are telling each other stories or asking after the baby's teeth or just laughing as they knock back another beer. Three-quarters through the speech the decibel level is so high that no one hears the Minister except the Minister, nor do they notice when he finishes.

After the speeches comes the real point of the evening, *The*

Waiting for business: parking attendant . . .

... *Fortune teller*

Fabulous Neptune Shows. According to the Oxford English Dictionary the word *fabulous* can mean *astonishing, incredible, unhistorical*. Those who run the Neptune must be keen readers of the Oxford Dictionary. Their *non-stop extravaganza* begins with a group of demure Chinese girls doing a Spanish dance, with a couple of young male Chinese shouting *Olé* and stamping their heels. Customarily, the central current of energy in Andalusian gypsy dancing is sex. The spark must crackle from male to female or else the whole performance struts into absurdity. It is not in the Chinese character to be publicly sexy, especially with breasts and arms. (The allurements of the *cheong-sam* are a mystery unto themselves.) These good girls whirl and stamp and shake their flat chests but good they remain, with not a red chili's-worth of gypsy wickedness.

Then come singers, in Chinese and English-American, and finally the formal dance troupe, Chinese, Malayan and Indian, in a romp from *Swan Lake*. Without a pause the orchestra suddenly switches to Budapest and a Hungarian *Czardas* is in slightly less than full swing. On it goes, the girls sprinting off stage and coming back just, or almost, in time to the music that has shifted to Naples, before dashing across the water to Greece. The girls are never quite in line or all kicking together. A young Indian who is watching leans over and says, *Self-expression, I think you could call it*.

Amateurish it may be, as well as fabulous, but there is nothing cold about the evening, not even the food. The Singapore National Identity may not quite know where it is going, but there is no doubt about the gusto with which it assimilates all the international ingredients.

The poet Edwin Thumboo (who, perhaps unexpectedly for such a good poet, happens also to be the Head of the Department of English Language and Literature in the University of Singapore) has written a poem called *Games* which expresses the omnivorous appetite of Singapore for every sort of foreign experience, not always of the best quality.

I approach the theatre
  They are playing Cousin Kate
I divert to the cinema
  They are screening Lawrence of Arabia
I retreat to the newspapers
  Princess Anne is speeding
I look for sarong and baju
  They sell Levis
I get to the drive-in
  Colonel Sanders is licking his fingers
I despair for a drink
  Get served Coca-Cola
I reach my friend
  He serves chilled Pepsi-Cola
I get home to my TV
  Steve McGarrett says:
  'Book 'em. Murder one'.

Edwin Thumboo might have added Christmas to the list. Singaporeans have cheerfully absorbed Christmas as the Chingay Procession absorbs girl pipers or Peter Pan. If you come to Singapore a fortnight before Christmas you find Mr. Frosty the cuddly snowman already installed in the foyer of most hotels, with a snow-hut in front of him with little plaster figures of Caucasian children outside, and a Santa Claus in a sled. Often there are Chinese family groups, and sometimes a wedding group, being photographed in front of the snow hut.

In a restaurant the waitresses are all little Miss Christmases, wearing red mini-dresses bordered with white fur that is apt to shed a whisker or two into the rice. Christmas dinner is advertised at the hotel for $105 a head, and that is not as expensive as in some other hotels. For this you get *Free 1 pint bottle French Champagne and novelties*. All this is in a country where there are only about 150,000 Christians (a figure which can be verified by looking in the official handbook, *Singapore Facts and Pictures*, under the heading *Culture and Recreation*).

The new mix of international ingredients is far more elegantly displayed in Jurong Township, which is not only ports and factories but housing and gardens and swimming pools. And people. In the decade from 1969–79 public housing units under the Jurong Council's management increased from 3,004 units to 23,289 units. The people who live in these units need to do more than work and live close to their work. Many of them learn, and not just at school. In typical Singapore style, huge industrial training centres have been set up in cooperation with businesses from various countries, e.g. the Tata Government Training Centre, the Japan-Singapore Training Centre, and the Rollei Government Training Centre.

The greatest contrast with Chinatown, Arab Street and so on is in the Chinese and Japanese Gardens at Jurong, which you reach by nimbly dodging between the joggers endlessly proceeding along the paths around Jurong Lake, to those curiously differing sounds of the soft thump of their feet and rasp of their breathing.

The audacity of Singapore's leaders is always impressive, but nowhere more so than in this whole concept of creating these vast Chinese and Japanese Gardens in the midst of an industrial development, allowing a kingly space of water, grass, flowers and trees, rocks and temples in between estates of high-rise housing and high-efficiency industry. You can even find lovers blissfully disregarding the discomforts of the thick planks and concrete of the benches hidden between the bushes and trees.

Singapore needs both the packed details of Chinatown and the uncluttered classical vistas of the Chinese and Japanese gardens. People like Goh Keng Swee made sure that these needs were fulfilled. One hopes that his successors will continue to recognize them.

The other stroke of audacity, of course, was to create a Japanese garden at all. One would think that the memories of the Japanese occupation, and the rival claims of the multi-racial Singapore society, would have suggested the planning of a Malayan or Indian garden rather than a Japanese. The decision was in fact symbolic of the confidence Singaporeans have in their national identity. The leaders' grasp of the national direction was strong enough for them to be able to think about expanding Singapore's interests rather than placating minorities. The Chinese now comprise 77 per cent of Singapore's population. Their dominance is obvious, but it is a power used for the benefit of the nation of Singapore, not for local Chinese nor for Chinese across the sea. The People's Action Party has always had representatives of the minorities in its leadership, and has always emphasized the importance of the minorities.

Chinatown is not Singapore, but it is also more than a symbol of Chinese culture. It is, as Mr. Yuen observed, a vital part of the *city life style, e.g. Arab Street, Serangoon Road, and the Muslim quarters*. When a nation has confidence in its history, then it has achieved identity.

Passerby, off Serangoon Road

Fortune teller, South Bridge Road

The Straits

The Johore Causeway connecting Singapore to the mainland of the Malay Peninsula seriously impairs Singapore's status as an island. It is not a bridge under which ships can go, but a sullen lump of rock and concrete and tar over which pour streams of cars and an occasional train. It is 1,000 metres long and was completed by the British in 1923 so the rubber and tin of Malaya could be channelled to Singapore. It also carries a major part of Singapore's water supply from the rivers of the Peninsula to the Island.

The best way to see it is to drive round through the giant new housing development called Woodlands, down a winding road to the edge of the Johore Straits, where there are usually a couple of cars parked by a little sweet and drink stall. Huge and black above you is the roaring Causeway, and the great silver water pipes, and across the still water, no wider than a big river, are the buildings of Johore Bahru. In the corner under the streaming traffic of the Causeway the waterfront is paradoxically calm and quiet, a little oil barge is beached by the snotty-nosed rocks lapped by a brown tide, and a fishing boat swings at anchor.

The Causeway is as full of meanings as a French symbolist poem. It has been a symbol of British Colonialism, which not only varied from one country to another but in the composition of the colonialists themselves. By the building of it in 1923 the unity of the Straits Settlements of Malaya and Singapore became one of land as well as water.

Today, across the Causeway, Johore Bahru and the new Singapore town of Woodlands look at each other, and it does not seem accidental that anyone driving south across the Causeway should have for a first sight of Singapore, above the low ground and muddy shore, the gleaming towers of planned and prosperous living. Drive north across the Causeway into Malaysia, and the skyline, pierced by a number of Singapore-like buildings, is dominated by the Istana Besar, the Sultan's Palace, with its 32 metre tower. Unbelievably, it was here that Lieutenant-General Yamashita had his headquarters in 1942; from the tower he could see the British and Australian troops on Singapore Island, and no doubt also note how almost nothing was being done to stop him from sending his army across the Straits of Johore. Later, a British prisoner of the Japanese, on being asked why this perfect observation tower had not been blown up or shelled, answered: *No one imagined any army commander would be so rash as to choose such an obvious target as his headquarters.*

On the night of the 30th and the early morning of 31 January 1942, 30,000 British and Australian troops marched over the Causeway while the two surviving pipers of the Argyll and Sutherland Highlanders piped them across to *Jennie's Black E'en* and *Bonnets over the Border*. Finally the remnants of the Argylls, who had made up the rearguard, were piped across to *Hielan' Laddie*. It was all done at night in secret, and the million-odd inhabitants of Singapore did not know that they were besieged on the Island. Then on the morning of 31 January, British Army engineers, with the help (ironically enough) of Lim Bo Seng's Quarry Workers' Union, blew a rather pathetic 50 metre breach in the Causeway, which anyone could walk across at low tide. The explosives had not knocked much of a hole in the Causeway, but symbolically the British Empire had been blown sky-high.

A little over 20 years later the Prime Minister of Malaya, Tunku Abdul Rahman, proposed the foundation of Malaysia in a Federation of Malaya, Singapore, Sarawak, Brunei and North Borneo, and in September 1962, 75 per cent of the electorate of Singapore voted in favour of a merger with Malaysia. A year later Singapore became fully independent within the Federation of Malaysia. Then in less than two years the Causeway was as it were blown up again, and on 9 August 1965 Singapore separated from Malaysia and became a Sovereign Nation. But, symbolically enough, Lee Kuan Yew and the People's Action Party were already busy building the Causeway up again, for an independent Singapore needed the trade and commodities of Malaysia as much as she did in the days of the Straits Settlements.

The Causeway has, in fact, especially at weekends, become a symbol for escape from the tiny island of ordered life that is Singapore, as cars full of people head for all the things that Peninsular Malaysia has to offer and which Singapore cannot provide: beaches not backed by high-rise buildings, where turtles lay their eggs, mountains and waterfalls, gambling, village crafts and dances. Peninsular Malaysia is a perpetual reminder of the penalty Singapore suffers for being the super-efficient city-state.

To the east of the Causeway, north of Kranji and the War Cemetery, is the coast where the Japanese came ashore to conquer Singapore, while Lieutenant-General Percival, in a mild and ineffectual way, was expecting them to land to the east of the Causeway. Follow the Straits of Johore east for a few kilometres and you come to the site of the British Naval Base. A little further, and aircraft are coming in over Pulau Seletar to land at Seletar aerodrome, the former RAF base. Go on to the tip of the Island and you are at Changi, where the prison gates closed on the British and Australian prisoners of Japan, and where the 15 inch naval fortress guns, with their armour-piercing shells, awaited the enemy that never came from the sea.

The south coast of Singapore Island, from Jurong to Katong, is one long success story of the sea, but the north coast is another, and very, British story.

It is impossible to understand Singapore without trying to assess the impact on it of the British, and the English language. Independence and Lee Kuan Yew's paradoxical pragmatic vision have only deepened the influence of both.

The ascendancy of the British is all the more remarkable since Singapore was multi-racial from its foundation. True, the British ran the place, but in an infinitely more haphazard and tenuous fashion than that in which they managed India; and there were very few of them. Although Singapore became a great base for the armed forces, it was never conquered or fought over. Nor was Malaya, apart from a few skirmishes in the States. Singapore and Malaya were prize examples of the process whereby so much of the 19th-century British Empire was marshalled in moods ranging from negligence to pique. Francis Light talked the British into taking over Penang. Raffles' eloquent letters persuaded them not to let Malacca go. Raffles bluffed the British into the establishment of Singapore. It is ironic that Yamashita, his troops almost out of ammunition and supplies, bluffed Percival into surrendering Singapore to the Japanese.

In 1852 Disraeli remarked in exasperation, *These wretched Colonies*

The Causeway: from Singapore

The Causeway: from Johore Bahru

will all be independent in a few years, and are a millstone around our necks. The Straits Settlements were not even colonies, and it took over 100 years to reach independence, but they certainly were millstones round the East India Company's neck. They were ruled from India through Penang as a Presidency until 1830 when they were demoted to a Residency responsible to the Presidency in Bengal. Singapore became the seat of Government in 1857. The so-called Governors were really only Residents, with a handful of bureaucrats scrambling together reports for Calcutta. Only a few officials could speak Malay, and none Chinese. The same year, the *Singapore Free Press* complained, *There is probably no other Government in the world so incapable of addressing the people as that of the Straits.*

By the 1860's, when the population of Singapore was over 80,000, 55,000 were Chinese and 13,000 Indian. The Malays had dropped back to third, and the British were, as always, a tiny minority. Yet even by the 1820's and '30's the British were already building in great style, thanks to an Irishman, George Drumgold Coleman, superintendent of Public Works, overseer of Convict Labour, and Land Surveyor. Convicts, mostly Indian, who were first brought from Bencoolen in 1825, were the hidden builders of Singapore, as they were of Sydney, that true convict colony. With them Coleman extended the seafront by reclaiming land and built North and South Bridge Roads. Coleman designed and built a number of magnificent houses, including one for himself in 1829, which later became the London Hotel and then slipped downhill into tenements until 1969, when, instead of being restored it was destroyed – an all-too-familiar Singapore pattern. The beautiful little Armenian Church, built in 1835, is Coleman's most notable surviving building.

Coleman no doubt would have liked to have designed many more public buildings, but there was no money available, Singapore being a free port whose merchants had no wish to be taxed. Besides, the East India Company had lost its monopoly of the China trade in 1834, making it even more parsimonious than usual. The best comment on Singapore's public buildings in Coleman's time comes from a visitor, George Windsor Earl, who wrote in *Eastern Seas*, published in 1837, *The town can boast of no*

Government buildings of any importance, with the exception of the jail, a square white building erected in a swamp at the back of the town.

The followers of the various religions had rather more faith in Singapore than the civil authorities. The first Christian churches were built in the 1830's; the fine Thiau Hok Keong Temple was built in the early 1840's, its exuberant ornaments and statues and pillars brought from China by Hokkien junk-owners; the elegant Mosque in Kampong Glam was built in 1846; various Indian temples were built in the 1850's and '60's. Christianity was always in a minority in Singapore, but the site of St. Andrews Anglican Cathedral near the Padang, in its own open space, makes it appear as if Singapore city were a part of the British Establishment's belongings. Like all British churches in the tropics, on its interior walls are sad tablets mourning those who died young or at sea or of disease, and in this case there is the added burden of the Japanese war. Perhaps the saddest of all the inscriptions is one to the memory of 41 Australian nurses.

The Singapore authorities are extraordinarily amiable about the visible heritage of the British past. They have allowed the British War Memorial not far from the Cathedral to remain, and all the street signs and names are in English. It is good that the names remain; they are mostly of Singapore's history, as is Coleman Street in which the Cathedral stands.

In the 19th century the inhabitants of the Straits Settlements were strictly distanced from the Britain in whose name they were governed; there were authorities in London, Calcutta and the Settlements themselves. The giant upheaval of the Indian Mutiny led finally to the Settlements being made a Crown Colony under the Colonial Office in 1867. The inevitable result of this was to end, more by expediency than by plan, the artificial situation whereby Penang, Malacca and Singapore existed without a hinterland, and where Malaya was not a country but a turbulent mixture of feudal states and ill-defined loyalties and borders. The British at home were scarcely aware of this. Their attitude is nicely summed up in a minute of Viscount Kimberley, Colonial Secretary in the 1870's, on a query about the Prussians wanting to use one of the islands off the East coast of Johore as a coaling station: *The first step is to ascertain distinctly where the Maharajah and his Islands are.* Their policy towards the Malay States was non-intervention; when the Duke of Buckingham was Colonial Secretary he wrote to Singapore to the Governor Sir Harry Ord that: *The true policy of the British Government of the Straits Settlements is not to attempt to control but to keep clear of, native disorder.*

The 'native disorder' was indeed formidable. Of the Malay States those to the north, Kedah, Kelantan and Trengganu were tributaries of Siam; Selangor was ruled by Bugis from Makassar, who had conquered it in the 17th century; Negri Senbilan had been created in the 18th century by Menangkabau princes from Sumatra. In addition to fratricidal wars amongst the Malay Rajas the Chinese, who had long been trading and working the highly profitable tin mines, were divided into feuding secret societies, as indeed was Singapore itself. Added to these troubles was piracy, a thriving industry encouraged by many a Raja tucked away in coastal rivers or on islands. No wonder the Chinese merchants of Singapore petitioned Governor Ord in 1873 that the British Government should intervene to establish stability in Malaya. *Hitherto*, they wrote, *there has been a large trade with the Native States of the Malay Peninsula, but owing to internal dissentions this has in some cases entirely ceased, Laroot, Perak and Selangor have been and are in a state of such disturbance, that all legitimate trade with them is at an end, and unless the British Government interfere to restore order and peace, these rich countries will be impoverished and their inhabitants ruined.*

In London Kimberley, with the help no doubt of a map, approved of these sentiments. He was also aware that Germany was interested in Malaya; hence the enquiry after that coaling station. The result was that under an unwilling Gladstone and then an enthusiastic imperialist Disraeli, the British Residents were gradually installed in the various Malay States, often, as Raffles had done at Singapore, by signing treaties with Sultans who were *de jure* rather than *de facto* rulers.

Perhaps the most remarkable of all the Residents was Frank Swettenham, who was criticized on his original appointment to Selangor for his youth and lack of experience, but eventually became the first Resident-General of the Federated Malay States

Armenian Church

Emerald Hill

and laid the foundations of modern Malaysia.

It was Swettenham who witnessed a classic meeting, that between Captain Speedy, Assistant Resident at Larut, and Walter Pickering, who arrived in Singapore in 1872 to take up his appointment as Chinese Interpreter. It was an historic appointment, for until Pickering's arrival, no British official had been able to talk any of the languages of the 100,000 odd Chinese in the Straits Settlements. Speedy was a rare exception who could manage a sort of Chinese. Pickering played the bagpipes, and took them with him wherever he went. *Speedy*, wrote Swettenham, *seemed surprised – and rather pained – to find that Pickering spoke Chinese with great ease and understanding, but when he discovered that he also played the bagpipes he became almost green with envy. He admitted that he had never met a man with those rare accomplishments, and he immediately set himself to learn the latter, claiming that he already had some knowledge of the Chinese tongue.*

Pickering's bagpipes exemplify the extraordinary capacity of the British to devote their lives to foreign races and yet keep themselves inimitably apart. To the end of his life he maintained that the Book of Proverbs contained more wisdom than Confucius, Mencius and all the Chinese sages combined, and that a translation of Shakespeare would *raise the character of our nation in the eyes of the conceited Chinese*. Yet he did more than any non-Chinese in Singapore's history to understand and help the Chinese, both in his initial appointment as Interpreter and his later one as Protector. They certainly needed protecting, more from themselves than anybody else. The Malays across the Johore Straits may have had quarrelling Rajas, but they had a basically normal and orderly society. Singapore was alarmingly abnormal. In the late 1890's, with a population of over 100,000 there was an appalling sexual imbalance: 85.8 per cent of the total population, and 93.5 per cent of the Chinese population, were males. Part of Pickering's job was to intercept the junk cargoes of boys being landed in Singapore to serve as male prostitutes and to arrange Registrars and Inspectors of female brothels, into which he was able to introduce some improvements of health and management, not without protests from the Madams who, Pickering recorded, came to the Protectorate *throwing back their license boards, dancing on the floors with wooden clogs and howling furiously*. Pickering's worst problem, however, no doubt intensified by sexual frustrations, was the violence engendered by the all-powerful Secret Societies. He believed in working through them, but Clementi Smith, the Governor (who was also a Chinese scholar), broke them up and suppressed them.

Gambling was another problem. Poor Pickering was attacked in his office by a frustrated gambler, a Teochew carpenter, who hit him on the forehead with the blunt end of an axe, *not to kill but merely to frighten him*. As it was, his brain was damaged and though he lived to the age of 67 he was never consistently well again.

Some of the greatest British contributions to Singapore, and to the Straits Settlements, were in the field of science, beginning with Raffles' establishment of a Botanic Garden (which for a long time did not fare too well). Where the Chinese and the Indians came to work and to make money, and the Malays were content to live, a few Englishmen came with this passion to extend scientific knowledge. One interesting visitor was a most remarkable Catholic priest from Australia, the Reverend Julian Tenison Woods, the author of 175 learned papers on geology, botany, zoology and marine biology, who arrived in Singapore in 1883 to stay with his friend Governor Weld.

A modest man, accustomed to working in his bedroom when not camping out in his wanderings in the wilds of Australia, he was amused at the splendours of Government House (built for Governor Ord in 1869, now the Istana). Writing to a friend he said, *The Governor sent out his launch to take us off the steamer, and met us at the landing, where we went to Government House as most magnificent swells, where the least of the footmen might be mistaken for a rajah at the lowest. I am now writing in my bedroom, which is a stone colonnade about 50 feet square and 30 or 40 feet high . . .*

Weld had just taken delivery of a huge new steam yacht, the *Seabelle*, with a crew of 45, which would enable him to visit the Malay States in suitable style, and they set off on this for Malacca, Selangor and Perak, where Father Woods was to carry out scientific expeditions on behalf of the Government.

In Perak a series of receptions had been arranged by Sir Hugh Low, the Resident. Woods described them to a friend: *Salutes, triumphal arches, dinners, reviews of troops, Malay, Hindu and Chinese dancers, theatre, fireworks and processions and everywhere the companies of Sikhs, the finest, handsomest men in the world . . .*

Father Woods went on to some intrepid explorations in the mountains and wrote some valuable reports, especially about further prospects of tin mining.

The Residents and Governors were often amateur scientists of sufficient quality to be able to communicate with visiting professionals. The adventurous and enthusiastic Governor Weld unfortunately retired just as some of the most interesting and influential of all the English scientists arrived in Singapore – among them, Henry Nicholas Ridley, who in 1888 became Director of the Gardens and Forests of the Straits Settlements at Singapore.

Raffles had brought a European gardener from Bencoolen to establish a Botanic Garden in 1819, in 19 hectares at the foot of Government Hill. Raffles planted cloves and nutmegs, and had firm ideas for an experimental garden that would lead to commercial development. However, as with his Institution, nobody had time to spare from making money to worry about botany or education, and the jungle took over the garden while the Institution fell into ruin. In 1859 a new garden at Tanglin, of about 32 hectares, was established by the Agri-Horticultural Society, whose ambitions for it included a bird-park, a zoo, a bandstand for concerts by the Regimental band, and a nursery which bred plants for members of the Society. It did not flourish, and in 1874 the Government took it over and developed its botanical and economic activities. In view of Ridley's later work, it was important that this commercial activity and organization already existed.

Ridley, who had already been on natural history expeditions to several countries in Europe and to Brazil and to the Island of Fernando Naronha, was chiefly attracted to that part of his duties which involved exploratory surveys in the Malayan forests.

But at Tanglin his main, and historic, enthusiasm was for *Hevea*

St. Andrew's Cathedral

Telok Ayer Market

Brasiliensis, the Para rubber tree. Sir Clement Markham and Sir Joseph Hooker, Director of the Royal Botanic Gardens at Kew, had instructed H.A. Wickham to bring 70,000 seeds to Kew in 1875. Despite Wickham's efforts to speed the project by feasting the Brazilian customs officers and filling them up with liquor, there were so many delays that only about four per cent of the seeds survived. From these, however, the Kew gardeners raised a sufficient number to send about 1,900 young plants in Wardian cases (a sort of miniature travelling greenhouse) to Ceylon and Singapore. Ridley inherited the survivors of these plants, and he knew about the rubber tree from his visit to Para in 1887. Within a few years he had worked out the herring-bone pattern of tapping the tree, by which the latex can be drained off without injuring the tree, and he was urging planters all over Singapore and Malaya to plant the trees. But they dismissed him as *Mad Ridley*, and Weld's successor, Sir Charles Mitchell, ordered Ridley to stop fiddling with 'exotic' plants, and even published a notice in the Government Gazette saying that the Para trees did not produce rubber!

It was a new invention, the motor car, and the demand for rubber for its tyres, that changed the landscape of Malaya and revolutionized its economy. 'Mad' Ridley's scorned seeds led to the expansion of the export of rubber from 104 tons in 1905 to 196,000 tons in 1914, more than half of the total supply in the world at that time.

Singapore profited greatly from the rubber boom, being first a channel for its export and then, after the establishment of a Rubber Association in Singapore in 1911, becoming a world marketing centre.

The first rubber plantation in Singapore was at Ponggol where the trees were planted in 1907. Other plantations in Singapore were of gambier (a plant used for tanning and dyeing) and pepper. But Ridley would not have approved of the destructive and haphazard abuse of the soil by the planters, who simply exhausted the soil and moved on. The worst hazard, however, was the tiger. So many cultivators were carried off by tigers that plantations were abandoned, and when the road was built to the top of Bukit

Timah a delicious *frisson* was given to ladies in the carriages by the roars of tigers in the nearby jungle. Fortunately this meant that no bungalows were built on Bukit Timah and led to its establishment as a forest reserve, where at least one small portion of the original Singapore jungle has been able to survive.

In 1843, an article in the *Free Press* said that *dark masses of primeval forest stretch away from Bukit Timah on every side*, and, where the Causeway now is, just a glitter of water could be seen through *the one continuous dark forest reaching to the distant hills of Johore*. The *Free Press* much doubted whether the whole of the Island would ever be cleared. Now it is only in the Bukit Timah reserve, and the parks around the reservoirs, that tropical nature can close around you, the high cicadas whirring even more loudly than the distant traffic, a butterfly passing a brown leaf swaying down to the hushed ground, while the air seems a living thing standing still.

The lonely British planter in the Malayan jungle, the general of his ranks of rubber trees, coming down on leave to drink gin slings at Raffles Hotel in Singapore, is as romantic a literary figure as Conrad's traders and pirates. Unfortunately he also often represented the bad side of the British character, as the Residents mostly exemplified the good. Planters were often arrogant, racist, and intellectually limited, and the women, especially, were intolerably spoiled by having so many servants and so little to do. The worlds of Raffles, Farquhar and Francis Light are still present in Conrad's novels and stories, in which the native peoples are always there, and often of great importance in the action. In Somerset Maugham's stories a 'native' or a 'Chinaman' hardly ever appears. Eurasians hide in the shadows of sex, and the world of *The Club* is central, where a member who marries a 'coloured girl' or a Eurasian has to resign.

Maugham's British are exiles; they may make a good show of running a plantation or a business, but the climate and the scenery are alien, they have no love for the people around them. Like Maugham himself, they lack resources, they have none of the scientific or artistic passions of the Residents, none of the central passion for the sea or the fascination of the mystery of the East present in Conrad's characters. An exception is Neil MacAdam in the story of that name. His employer, Captain Bredon, says, *There's nothing much to see in Singapore*; however, Neil is in ecstasies over the place. *It was outside, in the streets, that it was most thrilling, and except that he was a grave and sober young man he would have laughed aloud with joy. Everything was new to him. He walked till he was footsore.* He looks at the Chinese, the Bombay merchants, the Tamils, the Arabs, and he is confused. *He thought it would take him years to find his bearings in this multi-coloured excessive whirl.*

That last, vivid phrase is not one that would have been used by most of Maugham's characters. Moon, the retiring Resident of Timbang Belud, in *The Back of Beyond*, is a cold man who has enjoyed his power and his capacity for justice, and been even-handed to Malays, Chinese and white planters. Like Maugham himself, he thinks it odd that the protagonists of the story, *These commonplace people leading lives so monotonous, should have been convulsed by such a tragedy*. In another story a Resident named Featherstone seems an ordinary enough man until Maugham hears his story, which is one of incest; the girl he is engaged to is in love with her brother. But here, in the Residency, the surroundings of which have *almost the look of an English park*, Maugham senses that this ordinary and upright man is given some further quality by the jungle and the river. *I wondered whether, unbeknownst to him, the tender and yet strangely sinister aspect of the scene, acting on his nerves and his loneliness, imbued him with some mystical quality, so that the life he led, the life of the capable Administrator, the sportsman, and the good fellow, on occasion seemed to him not quite real.*

The collision with reality, for these people living in such a taut society, is almost always represented by a sexual disaster, the volcano of adultery, or worse. The worst is in *The Letter*, when the woman finds out that her lover has long had a Chinese mistress, a fat woman older than she, to compound the villainy. She reviles and insults him, and when he finally tells her that the Chinawoman was *the only woman who really meant anything to him* she shoots him.

The most touching of all Maugham's stories about this situation, brilliant in its economy and lack of moralizing, is *Masterson*. Although set in Burma it could just as well be in Malaya

Business centre

Recreation centre

or Singapore. Masterson lives with a Burmese woman, by whom he has had two children. She is beautiful, amiable, intelligent, faultless. She asks him to marry her but he will not. Eventually she leaves him, but although his life is empty without her he still will not marry her. The reason is: '*I tell you. If I married her I would have to stay in Burma for the rest of my life.*' Masterson is devoted to Burma; he has amassed a fine collection of Burmese arts and crafts. But he goes on to say, '*I'm happy enough here, but I don't want to live here always, I couldn't. I want England. Sometimes I get sick of this hot sunshine and these garish colours. I want grey skies and a soft rain falling and the smell of the country . . . it's a dream if you like, but it's all I have, it means everything in the world to me, and I can't give it up.*'

Singapore owes its modern existence to the English, but this extraordinary detachment, this devotion to a dream (Masterson knows he will just be a rather fat silly outsider when he goes home), has had profound effects on Singapore's history.

Masterson's dream is doubly threatened by this Burmese girl he has lived with and treated as a wife, and given everything he would give a wife, except the bond of marriage. The racism of the 1920's and '30's forbids him taking an Asian wife to England. His Englishness also renders him incapable of admitting the possibility of love between him and the Burmese girl; all his capacity for love must be given to his dream of England. The whole power of the story lies in the appalling failure of this nice chap to regard her as a whole human being; she remains Burmese, he English. '*I rather admire her. I had no idea she had so much character. Sometimes I'm awfully inclined to give way.*' He hesitated for a little while. '*I think, perhaps, if I thought she loved me I would. But of course, she doesn't; they never do, these girls who go and live with white men. I think she liked me, but that's all.*'

In a recent novel, *The Singapore Grip* by J.G. Farrell, set in the 1940's, the isolation exists even in Tanglin, the most respectable suburb of Singapore. *If you looked more closely you would see that it was a suburb ready to burst at the seams with a dreadful tropical energy.* Even the people's orderliness is like the hands of a clock and *that ordered life in Tanglin depended in the same way on the city below, and on the mainland beyond the Causeway, whose trading, mining and plantation concerns might represent wheels and cogs, while their mute, gigantic labour force are the springs, steadily causing pressure to be transmitted from one part of the organism to another.*

The British Administrators and scientists who contributed so much to Singapore and Malaya were always conscious of, indeed they lived by, the interconnection of the wheels and cogs and the hands, but the downfall of the British came from those who thought that they alone could control time. In fact, as they soon learned, their time had come.

For those in authority in London, Singapore became something quite different from that peaceful trading centre envisaged by Raffles. The haphazard British Empire had been accumulated for reasons of trade, or expediency, such as the dumping of convicts, and kept secure by the British navy. Suddenly after 1914 it began to assert itself in terms of strategy, particularly in the Indian and Pacific oceans. Like the sleeping Gulliver who awoke to find himself tied down by Lilliputians, the British giant was bound to the globe by shipping lanes, by the threads of navigation running to London from Sydney, Melbourne, Auckland, Hong Kong, and a hundred other ports. But unlike Gulliver, Britain could not burst free of these threads; by negligently assembling her Empire she was bound to it.

The defence needs of the Empire clashed with the enthusiasm for disarmament that followed 1918. Britain, the U.S.A., Japan and France, by the Naval Limitation Treaty of 1922, agreed to regard the Pacific as an area of peace where no new bases would be built, and the size of navies would be reduced. This meant that, in the event of a crisis, warships would have to be sent all the way from London. They would need a base for docking and repairs and Singapore was the obvious choice, especially as it was just outside the area specified in the Limitation Treaty. In fact, the decision had already been made, in 1921 at the Imperial Conference, to go ahead with the building of a base at Singapore.

The notion that there seems to have been some logic in all this is easily dispelled by a glance at what actually happened, and at the almost total lack of understanding in London of the 'East' and of Australia and New Zealand. The British on the spot in Singapore and Malaya were a complex mixture of devoted experts and arrogant opportunists interested only in making money. In London there were only armchair strategists, even if they had names like Churchill. None of them went to Singapore, let alone Japan or Australia. No one understood the implications of the tenuous hold that the British had in Singapore and Malaya. No one attempted to assess the extent of Japanese brains, efficiency and pride.

In 1925 the British Foreign Secretary Austen Chamberlain said, *I cannot conceive of any circumstances in which, single handed, we are likely to go to war with Japan.* In the same year, Winston Churchill, Chancellor of the Exchequer, said there was *absolutely no danger of a sudden crisis.* Singapore was not to be thought of in connection with Japan, but only as a main line of communications with Australia. *I do not think in our lifetime or in that of our children you are going to see an attempt by Japan to invade or colonise Australia by force.*

The first suggestions for building a naval base in Singapore had been in the 1880's and '90's, when the fears were of Russia and France. In 1902 the British signed a defensive pact with Japan, which lasted amicably for 20 years. In 1922 the Treaty was not renewed, because it might give offence to the U.S. and China. Japan was deeply offended, and so by 1925, when Austen Chamberlain and Winston Churchill were delivering their sentiments about peaceful Japan, it should surely have been clear that the only possible enemy in the East was in fact Japan, England's former staunch ally. Moreover, Japan could not have been pleased at the building of a great base at Singapore, 1,600 kilometres closer to Japan than Pearl Harbour.

In the event of a war in the East, if the Royal Navy were to be sent out to defend the Empire, then the British home waters in the Mediterranean would be left defenceless. If there were a war big enough for the Singapore base to be needed, then there would be no British warships to spare to use it.

The next absurdity was the building of a huge airfield and RAF base at Seletar, to defend the non-existent naval base. It was not supplied with enough aircraft to defend a fishing fleet.

The final absurdity was that in Conservative mood the British wanted the Singapore base, in Labour mood they did not. In 1923

Shifting earth, Woodlands

Moving islands, Marina City

85

Ramsey MacDonald said, *There is one colossal folly for which the Government must be made very seriously responsible, and that is the wild and wanton escapade of Singapore.* In 1924 MacDonald won the election and stopped work in Singapore. In November of the same year the Conservatives under Baldwin ousted him and work began again. Nothing much had been done except draining the swamps before MacDonald was back in 1929, and work was stopped again. In 1931 Japan invaded Manchuria and work began again. Then in 1937 Japan invaded China and work was actually speeded up, and the King George VI dry dock was opened in 1938.

For the British, the Naval Base and Seletar were the strangest homes away from home. It is an extraordinary experience today, in Singapore, to visit Seletar, which is both a Republic of Singapore Air Force base and a general aviation airport. You are stopped at the gate by smart sentries and asked your business. Having obtained permission to proceed, you are plunged into acute schizophrenia. You are still on Singapore Island, and yet you are driving down Piccadilly, or Regent Street, or Battersea Road. The barracks and buildings look as British as the names, and the only certainty is that millions of pounds must have been spent in building this monumental folly.

Seletar did not cost as much as the Naval Base (no one seems to know how much that was, at least 60 million pounds), but if the Naval Base was a white elephant, Seletar was the equivalent of the Great Auk. By the time it was needed it was as good as extinct, and might just as well have been used for housing squadrons of cavalry. Those in authority in London had no notion that the age of the aeroplane had arrived by the 1930's. If war should break out in the East, a relief naval force could arrive in 70 days, and of course Singapore, *a new, bigger and better Gibraltar, one of the most formidable concatenations of naval, military and strategic power ever put together*, as John Gunther ineptly described it in *Inside Asia* in 1939, would have no difficulty in holding off the attacker, who of course would be coming from the sea and from the South. (When war broke out in Europe the 70 days extended to an unbelievable 180.)

The British continued to send experts out to Singapore and then ignore their findings. Sometimes the experts later forgot their own advice. In 1937 the General Officer Commanding, Malaya, Major-General William Dobbie, and his senior staff officer, Lieutenant-Colonel Arthur Percival, carried out a planning exercise based on the premise that the Royal Navy was still steaming towards Singapore while the Japanese were attacking down the Malayan Peninsula. Dobbie, agreeing with Percival, wrote in a memorandum: *It is an attack from the northward that I regard as the greatest potential danger to the fortress.* (The planners of Singapore 'fortress' seem to have ignored both history and geography and pretended that Singapore could be considered quite separately from Malaya, and even that the fortress could be considered quite separately from Singapore Island.) Percival's imaginary Japanese attack could have been a blueprint for the one he had to meet in reality five years later when he was in command.

In November 1940 Air Chief Marshall Sir Robert Brooke-Popham, 62 and retired, was appointed Commander-in-Chief of land and air forces in the Far East. He had no powers over the navy or over coordination with Civil Defence and Administration. He reported that: *The defence of Singapore is not a question of holding on to an isolated fortress, which is only of value in itself, but of ensuring that a naval base can be used by His Majesty's ships . . . and we must combine the resisting power of an army with the striking power of an air force.* The Chief of Staffs' essential requirements were put at 336 first line aircraft. A Tactical Appreciation by local commanders in Singapore and Malaya put the total at 566 first line aircraft. Singapore had 48, with 13 in reserve, and no fighters. It is the final irony that London should have appointed an Air Chief Marshall to command an almost wingless body.

On the one hand the British wanted Malaya and Singapore to be the Allies' greatest suppliers of tin and rubber. On the other they had this absurd picture of *Fortress Singapore*, after England the main bastion of the Empire. Not only was it not armed as a fortress should have been, but it was vulnerable in a way that the British do not seem to have noticed until the worst happened. Singapore, with an inevitable influx of refugees in time of war, was a city of over a million people, not only vulnerable in themselves to air bombardment but dependent for survival, after the reservoirs had been used up, on the water pipes coming across the Causeway. The people of London, and perhaps some in Singapore too, seemed actually able to believe that there were two Singapores, one a fortress, the other a city, and that war would attack one, not the other. When the truth was dawning, Winston Churchill, in one of those moments when rhetoric and reality coincided, at last saw Singapore whole: *The hideous spectacle of the almost naked Island.*

The U.S. fleet did not arrive to save the Far East because it was at the bottom of Pearl Harbour. Most of the few aircraft in Malaya and Singapore, pathetic Wildebeestes, Wirraways and Buffaloes, were destroyed on the ground. The *Prince of Wales* and the *Repulse* were sent out by Churchill against all advice to create *a vague, potential menace.* After they had been sunk, Churchill said, *In all the war I never received a more direct shock . . . the efficiency of the Japanese in air warfare was at this time greatly underestimated both by ourselves and by the Americans.*

Churchill's portrait hangs in a place of honour in the Tanglin Club in Singapore, as it does in many similar institutions in Australia. Yet Churchill's ignorance settled the fate of Singapore, as his attempt to divert Australia's only fighting force of soldiers to the East might have done the same for Australia. Churchill's honesty after the event does not excuse his grotesque ignorance of the fact that Singapore had no defences to the North. *I ought to have known. My advisors ought to have known and I ought to have asked. The reason I had not asked is that the possibility of Singapore having no landward defences no more entered my mind than that of a battleship being launched without a bottom.*

As for the *fortress*, the great Naval Base, it was abandoned by the navy even before the exhausted troops who had been retreating down the peninsula were withdrawn across the Causeway.

The worst error of all, in the long catalogue of Churchill's failures to understand the reality of Singapore, is exposed in his cable of 10 February 1942 to Field Marshall Wavell, Supreme Commander in the Far East. *There must at this stage be no thought of saving the troops or sparing the population. The battle must be fought to the bitter end at all costs. Commanders and senior officers should die with their troops . . . the honour of the British Empire and of the British Army is at*

Dry land, East Coast

Dry dock, Sembawang Shipyard

stake. With the Russians fighting as they are and the Americans so stubborn at Luzon the whole reputation of our country and our race is involved. The next day Yamashita's troops occupied Bukit Timah.

Churchill's rhetoric is not all that far removed from Masterson's dream of England: *Our country . . . our race.* But multiracial Singapore was a city, wide open to attack, and the population *not to be spared* was Chinese, Malayan, Indian, far more than it was British.

If you fly east from the Causeway along the Straits of Johore, you pass the old Naval Base, then Seletar airport, then Punggol and come to Changi and the north-eastern end of Singapore Island.

The three stages of British rule are there beneath you: the Causeway, connecting Singapore to the Peninsula and the Straits Settlements; the Naval Base and Seletar, symbols not of Britain's might but her weakness; and Changi, symbol of her humiliation.

Changi prison, three kilometres towards Singapore city from Changi village, has within its walls only a part of the complex that formed the wartime internment camp. The Prison Chapel can be visited. You knock, knuckles never seeming more flimsy, on a huge steel door between the columns under the cupolas, which give it an air slightly like the entrance to a temple, except for the great letters in front of you: *Changi Prison*. An eye comes to a barred peephole. You are led to a glass window where you surrender your passport on a sliding tray. A guard takes you to a barred gate, which is not unlocked until the first barred gate is locked. Then you go down a barred alleyway by a little garden and up the stairs to the Chapel. The guard stays by the door while you look at the memorials and the photographs, the A.I.F. and British Army insignia and the battalion plaques; the photographs of Barrack Square, 17,000 men in an area 250 yards by 150 yards. It looks so ramshackle, like a bazaar. There is not really much to see in the Chapel, but it is a symbol of the little chapels the men built, around the Prison yards, and of the whole enormity of the war that seems so remote both from the peaceful surroundings of the Prison and the little garden, like a cloister, outside the windows. There is also a certain remoteness, of a different kind, from the few political prisoners that remain in Changi.

The Chapel is more than a shrine to suffering; it is also a memorial, and surely in this case a thankful one, to the end of white supremacy. It is also perhaps a reminder of how Japan missed her chance, in ending that supremacy, of uniting the peoples in the territories she conquered. Liberation was not a word that could be used about Japanese rule, but it is envisaged in that extraordinarily interesting little booklet issued to Japanese troops before the south-eastern campaign, *Read This and the War can be Won*. In the section headed *A hundred million Asians tyrannised by 300,000 whites* the writer goes on to say, *Once you set foot on the enemy's territories you will see for yourselves, only too clearly, just what this oppression by the white man means. Imposing, splendid buildings look down from the summits of mountains or hills on to the tiny thatched huts of natives. Money squeezed from the blood of Asians maintains these small white minorities in their luxurious mode of life – or disappears to the respective home-countries.*

These white people may expect, from the moment they issue from their mothers' wombs, to be allotted a score of natives as their personal slaves. Is this really God's will?

The reason why so many peoples of the Far East have been so completely crushed by so few white men is, fundamentally, that they have exhausted their strength in private quarrels, and that they are lacking in any awareness of themselves as a group, as peoples of Asia.

The humiliation of the whites by the Japanese created that awareness as never before, but the Japanese went too far, creating a backlash of sympathy in peoples who remembered the 'oppression' of the whites as being preferable to the tyranny of the Japanese. Ten years later oppression by the Communists, the immediate prospect of murder and rioting, and the further outlook of a closed and alien society, also united people in *their awareness of themselves as a group*, both in Malaya and Singapore. The arrival of General Templer to command the Emergency in Malaya provided an example of a type of Englishman never seen before in the area: dynamic, ruthless, efficient, and with the power to further the plan for independence for the native peoples of the Malaysian Peninsula.

Modern Singapore, created by the British, abandoned by the British, and set free by the British, continues to use the most priceless gift of the British, the English language. The two dominant official languages are Mandarin and English, and Mandarin has still only a rather shaky hold. But one has only to cross the Causeway to notice what one might have just accepted, that a majority in Singapore speak English, but that far fewer do in Malaysia.

The Causeway is vital, and is the symbol of Singapore's connection to the mainland of South-East Asia, but the strongest heritage of the British is not in stone or concrete, history, names and laws, but in English, the international language that is the basis of the prosperity of the international Island of Singapore.

High-rise: night

High-rise: day

A new life

It is a Chinese New Year party on the 14th floor of a high-rise block of apartments.

How do you like our Air Con? The host, a jolly man in a batik shirt, opens out his hospitable hands, each holding a can of Anchor Beer. It is just as he says: a cool breeze rushes through the wide-open windows and sliding doors and the curtains dance to a different sort of concrete music. How much more free and cheerful, this wind through the concrete towers, than the discreet rumble of the mechanical air-conditioner! And how much cheaper! And energy-saving! And healthy! One sees the wise leaders of Singapore nodding their heads, and even Lee Kuan Yew letting slip a smile.

And the open window, the suicide's ever-present, loaded, cocked gun, presents no threat at all, only a view through the other towers of Singapore's green sections and the perpetual travelling circus of tropical clouds.

The miniature high-rise tower of red and gold envelopes, the children's *ang pows*, flutter in the breeze by boughs of pussy willow shoots that have come all the way from China. In recesses in the walls there are big murals of incised and painted styrene plastic, designed by the host. Everyone is nibbling at the food that covers the central table: hard-boiled pigeons' eggs, sea-weed jellies, durian cakes. (Durian, that clumsy great rough fruit, is such a delicacy to those that love it, and to others it is the original bad smell that might be compared to the garlic breath of a Parisian labourer on the early morning Metro, rosewater mixed with Bols gin, or diesel oil washed with lavender soap.)

The two-bedroom apartment is full of relations, but though it is a family party, they find room for two New Zealanders and two Australians. A baby crawls towards the pussy willows. Mother-in-law in the kitchen doles out another dish of her superb spicy green pickles. Granny presides over her speciality, garnished noodles. *'Why does that chicken taste so good?' 'I rub the skin with paw-paw and only fry it for a very few minutes.' 'You've finished your beer. More beer here, more beer.'*

The Indian brother-in-law, a big, handsome man, sits forward in his chair with his arms curved so that his little son, with that delicious mixture of the sturdy and the tottering, can cannon off his arms instead of crashing into the little table which is covered with nuts. The sister-in-law, who manages a large firm and travels every year to Europe, is tall and elegant in jade green silk and her rope of jade beads and pendant is so heavy that even the host's Air Con cannot shake it. No one is tired, though they were up late celebrating New Year's Eve, and they all work long hours. The hostess, a young secretary at Jurong, rises daily at 5.30 to be ready for the journey that takes at least an hour or twice as long if somewhere along the way the road is blocked by a car, a fallen tree or a bus half-way down a storm drain. The baby, nearly a year old, spends the weekdays with a foster-mother and the weekends with his parents. It does not seem to suit him, he is edgy and nervous, unlike the little Indian boy who plays with a ball in the centre of a group of six, and is only bewildered when a two-year-old Chinese boy accidentally delivers a stupendous kick of the ball into his face. The two-year-old rushes over, most concerned, and is very gentle with the baby. The eight-year-old girl is in morning school, which means that she starts at seven and finishes at one, so the afternoon school can begin at 1.30. In the afternoon she practises her languages and does her homework.

Very useful daughter, says the printer, arriving with more beer. *She teaches her Hokkien father Mandarin.* He turns back to watch the international tennis on the t.v.

The shrine at the end of the room, hung with red and gold messages, Chinese oranges and pears beneath it, and the family milling all through the apartment were the traditional bases of Chinese life: religion and family. But in the high-rise it is Mandarin and English, education and discipline, to go higher in the world than the 14th floor. The flat belongs to the host and his wife (or at least they are paying it off), and thanks to the Central Provident Fund and the company pensions they will be millionaires when they retire at 50.

The intrinsic shape of Chinese New Year is conducive to looking ahead: there is nothing desperate, no 'Ring out the Old, Ring in the New' haste, for the sensible and pragmatic Chinese take a whole fortnight for their New Year. Even their greeting is subtle – *Gong Xi Fa Cai, Kong Hee Fatt Choy* – 'A Happy New Year' however you spell it, but not however you say it, for you have to have the right rising and falling inflection, otherwise all is confusion for the hearer.

At another flat, at another party, in a three-storey building around the courtyard, souvenirs of travels are mounted high on the walls, candles burn around offerings. Everyone moves softly because all shoes have been left outside the door. This time it is Tiger Beer, and more nuts, and irresistible slices of dried pork, and the food on the central table is covered with a white cloth until all the friends and relations have arrived, and then the cloth is whisked off and hours of chopping and mixing and flavouring become minutes of flashing chopsticks.

The Chinese, accused by writer Alex Josey of having no humour, are all laughing, but of course laughter may not be humour. However, listen to one of them who works for the big air-conditioning firm (there is only conventional air-conditioning in this three-storey apartment), but makes his big money supplying American garbage trucks to Singapore and Malaysia. He is talking about his fellow-Chinese, sending them up with that delicacy only possible for a man with a sense of humour, who loves what he is talking about. He says the Chinese are always so mercenary, so business-like, even in religion where they will make gifts to the gods at the temple but also give the same amount to the devils just in case. Yet these business-like people are such terrible gamblers. (*'Worse than Australians?' 'Yes, even worse than Australians.'*) Soccer only exists because everyone wants to bet on it, the taxi-driver will play the match game by the hour, a game even simpler than Australian two-up, consisting of guessing how many matches there are in a hand. Women who do not have to work will start playing mah-jong at 8.30 in the morning. There are lotteries, there is horse-racing, but no casino.

If one thing amuses him it is to hear Americans or Australians carrying on about the philosophical soul of the Orient, since he feels there is nobody so materialistic as the Chinese. He doesn't think much of the mainland Chinese either. They are very lazy, they have no motivation and they are certainly not more cultured than the overseas Chinese.

Fantastic

Iconoclastic

He adds that there are many traditions, however, that do survive. There is nothing unusual in a taxi-driver's son being high up in the Government of Singapore. It is an old Chinese custom: the gardener's son could marry the Emperor's daughter.

The businessman says that the true nature of Singaporeans is one of qualified arrogance. They are arrogant that they have survived so many crises and have made such a success of such an impossible situation (even Lee Kuan Yew once said that Singapore could not survive as a separate nation), but their arrogance is qualified by the knowledge of how frail it all is, how precarious, and how much they need to learn from other people.

Someone is looking at the paper. On the back page is a picture and a paragraph about Lee Tee Tong, who has just been released from confinement on Pulau Ubin. He is a union leader and Barisan Sosialis Communist who has been jailed since 1963. Dr. Lim Hock Siew was released two years ago after 15 years' gaol. The businessman says, *Five or six years ago maybe 60 per cent of people would have said, 'How tough that they were gaoled'. Now 90 per cent will say it was a jolly good thing.*

The satirical animation of his wife's face is not due to a different political opinion; she has been wrestling with melon seeds, nipping off the hard covering with her even teeth and eating the centre. She gives up. *What the hell. My mother told me that this was a good thing to do.* You *try some. I am giving up.*

Her husband has some final thoughts about Singapore and the Chinese. '*For Chinese, the two most important things are money and face. The one sometimes you can see; by the other you are always seen*'. He goes on to sum up Singapore. '*The most important achievement of Singapore has not been the economic miracle, education, the high-rise buildings, the clean-and-green story, the industrial development, but tolerance*'. '*Not for Communists*', someone murmurs. '*No, not for Communists. No, tolerance of each other, of different races and different styles of life and customs*'.

Some of the styles are pretty high. The two men across the table are talking about the high cost of golf. One of them is Secretary of a little golf club, one of the cheapest, the entry fee being only (S)$5,000. The most expensive clubs are around (S)$40,000, others about (S)$15,000. It is reported that newly elected members often sell their membership at a considerable profit to rich Japanese businessmen.

Yet this is a socialist country, with a paternalistic Government committed to the welfare of the workers and actually demanding from business an *increase* in wages. It is a sort of Mercedes Benz-socialism. There must be more Mercedes cars in Singapore than anywhere else in the world except West Germany.

* * *

The high-rise apartment houses are the dominating feature of the new mix of Singapore. The daily reality is of a life that has to be planned and synthetic – synthetic in the true general sense of the word, *the putting together of parts or elements so as to make up a complex whole*. What is immediately striking is that the great concrete blocks of flats look like simple statements of the way life is now; they do not look complex like a *kampong* with the house up on stilts, through which run chickens, while the dog sleeps under the tree whose branches brush the wooden verandah, and mosquitoes hum around the open toilet. Nor do they look complex like Chinatown, where the gaping shop-houses are full of stores downstairs and mysteries upstairs, where the whole exterior of the house writhes with ornament. And in both *kampong* and Chinatown all ages are mixed up together. About the only thing Chinatown and the high-rise seem to have in common is those clothes drying on poles stuck out from the windows.

But the high-rise is far more complex in the sum of its parts than even the *kampong* or Chinatown could be. In one great block all the races are mixed up together; Chinatown even has different quarters for different Chinese groups. There is a different story from everyone who lives high over Singapore. One teenage girl loves it because she can work without any interruptions instead of having the whole street surging in and out of her tiny house. A young couple are happy because they are tired of those famous benefits of the extended family and long for the privacy of the much-maligned nuclear family. The hired-car driver says, *Some things I like, but mostly I hate it*. He and his family had two acres, with fruit trees and chickens, that were taken over by the new Changi Airport. They were paid (S)$15,000 compensation for the trees and (S)$90,000 for the land. *That sounds a lot?* He laughs. *This car I drive, Mercedes 230, if I wish to buy a new one it cost me (S)$112,000*. He says their flat is very comfortable, very modern, very clean, very convenient, there is even room service as in a hotel. But there are so many charges for so many services that his family did themselves at the *kampong*. And his father, it was all sad for his father. He was an opium addict, and with all the new charges he could not afford his opium any more. Even worse, he had nothing to do, no trees to prune, no chickens to look after; he died within a year of moving from the *kampong*.

Two men who work together in the same enterprise, but live in different high-rise blocks, both say they like living in the high-rise, not only for the usual reasons of cleanliness and convenience, but also, surprisingly enough, for the presence of lots of neighbours. (Most people say you don't ever know who your neighbours are in high-rise.) One of them puts forward the hypothesis that Lee Kuan Yew is enthusiastic for high-rise because it enables the Government to destroy many of the people's traditions and customs, and thus to offer them new loyalties. This, says the man, is one of many lessons the Prime Minister has learned from the hated Communists.

Children's games and traditions suffer from the move to the high-rise. One of Singapore's writers, Chandran Nair, says he can remember all sorts of children's games and activities that are no longer possible. When he was a boy there were six different kinds of fish in Bukit Timah Creek; children caught butterflies and collected birds' eggs; they organized fights between spiders and scorpions – to mention but a few activities.

A prize-winning poem by Jillian Scully from the first Ministry of Culture Poetry Writing Competition is on a similar theme.

Urban congestion

Suburban flow

101

Where shall I find the spiders?

*My Dad says
He used to find them
in special bushes,
hiding between the leaves.*

*My Dad says
You must be quick
to put them in your tin,
or else they'll hop away.*

*My Dad says
It is fun to make them fight,
to own a winner,
to have a champion spider.*

Where shall I find the spiders?

*I know what to do,
I have my tin ready.
But where are the leaves, the bushes
in my high-rise concrete jungle?*

*In my flat there are spiders.
They are big ones
which I thought would fight.
I was sure I had my pick.*

*My Dad says
They are no good,
They'll never fight,
and he is always right.*

Where shall I find the spiders?

Given Singapore's geography and urban density, there seems to be no alternative to the high-rise. But that depends on the expert you are talking to.

The bureaucrats on top – Mr. Au Eng Kok, general manager for the Urban Redevelopment Authority, and Mr. Liu Tai Ker, chief executive of the Housing & Development Board – are, like all such people in Singapore, extraordinarily impressive. They are intelligent, direct and approachable, they are young and look fit, they do not exude that international smugness of the bureaucrat who knows he has the power to slow anything down, foul everything up, and cause the maximum of frustration to the maximum of people. These Singapore bureaucrats are of a different breed. They get things done. They are constantly calling for reports about the reactions of ordinary people to their actions. They undoubtedly mean well. But of course, at times, they may also be wrong.

Take Chinatown, for instance. It seems to be an essential part of Singapore, both for those who live there and for those who visit Singapore. At the extremely efficient Tourist Promotion Board they will give you the awesome statistic that the average tourist spends 2.6 days in Singapore: one day recovering from arriving; one day for shopping; and .6 of a day seeing Chinatown.

But at the same time the tourists can see the bulldozers biting bigger and bigger pieces out of Chinatown, and over the tiled and untidy roofs they can see the precise and slotted outlines of the new high-rise buildings that have gone up a few streets away. The authorities cannot keep Chinatown going just as a museum. It can only work, both for itself and for tourists, as a living entity. But if no one wants to live there? Mr. Au says fewer and fewer young people want to stay in Chinatown and who can blame them, for the overcrowding and lack of amenities are horrendous. One cannot defend a form of housing where families have to take it in turns, sometimes in three shifts in 24 hours, to sleep in cubicles that have no windows.

Mr. Lim Kim Guan, who takes visitors around Chinatown and knows it backwards, and who can point out a building of three-storey houses where more than 500 people live, admits that neither he nor his sons live in Chinatown.

Of course the high-rise has its limitations too, acknowledged by its most ardent defenders. The Singapore climate means that creepers and flowers cannot be allowed to hang down the walls of the buildings, as they do so agreeably in Rumania, for instance. Here the humidity would cause mould and decay in the walls. Pot plants would also be dangerous; they might fall off and kill someone down below. (They seem to take that risk in Rumania.) The corridors and breezeways that are necessary for cooling and for children to play in are admittedly noisy. The reason that the lifts stop only on alternate floors is purely economic (you always pick the floor above, so you only have to walk *down*). It saves a lot of dollars. It also means that girls are molested in the stairways.

If children go downstairs to play in the yards or just ride around on tricycles on the ground floor between the pylons, then the parents cannot see what is happening to them. Take a typical report from the *Straits Times*. *A sweeper . . . was jailed six months by a magistrate's court yesterday when he pleaded guilty to outraging a 9-year-old girl's modesty.*

The court heard that the girl was riding a tricycle with two of her friends on the ground floor of a block of flats in Kim Tian Road on Saturday when [he] approached them, saying that he would take each of the girls for a ride on his bicycle.

When it came to the girl's turn, he took her to a nearby multi-storey car park and used criminal force on her. He was arrested by a policeman on rounds.

And poverty can reduce the H.D.B. 1-room flat to an isolated squalor that is even worse than Chinatown. Take one example from Riaz Hassan's book (published in 1977), *Families in Flats*, of a former lorry-driver, now a street-sweeper, who was deserted by his wife and left with seven children.

The flat which Mr. C. and his children occupy is, perhaps, one of the most squalid in that particular block of flats. It is in a state of disrepair, primarily because Mr. C. cannot afford to pay the costs of repairing the wear and tear the flat is subjected to through intensive use by his children. The walls of the flat, which were once green, are now soiled and stained both by grease and by pencil marks. The floor of the flat, which is covered

Exterior: elevator

104

Interior : escalator

by a cracked sheet of linoleum that has seen better days, is littered with waste paper, sweet wrappers, and grains of rice from previous meals, which the housekeeping efforts of the children (conducted intermittently) have overlooked. The flat contains a bare minimum of furniture, reflecting the relatively low ability of the family to acquire material possessions . . . Throughout the entire flat, the atmosphere is dark and stuffy and reeks of stale urine emanating from the latrine (which is seldom washed) mixed with the smell of kerosene from the stove.

Such poverty might be more bearable in the company of Chinatown, but as a banana-seller interviewed by Riaz Hassan puts it, *Living in an H.D.B. flat is like being born of certain parents — you have no choice. You cannot choose your parents . . . you cannot choose where to live also. Nowadays where else can you live, I ask you? The rent for other kinds of housing is so high, that even if you can find a house . . . you can afford . . . who knows? . . . maybe it will be torn down so that more flats can be built.*

Some of Riaz Hassan's interviewees' comments do not speak too highly for high-rise living. *I noticed the facilities for children were almost nil. The community centre was too far away for the parents' liking and the children usually played along the sterile, dim corridors. People of different races (Chinese, Indian and Malay) live together in the same block of flats. This is a measure adopted by the H.D.B. to integrate the different racial groups so that prejudice will be eradicated. From the interviews, I found that language barriers still existed among the different racial groups. Most of the Chinese housewives claimed that they did not understand the languages of the Indian and Malay families. It was clear that there was not much social interaction among the different racial groups. Hence integration of the different racial groups was hindered to some extent.* On the other hand, another interviewer said, *I think H.D.B. flats enhance racial harmony between various groups. Although there is still some clustering of people of the same dialect or racial group, it is also true that, within one block of flats, one is exposed, more than before, to people of different ethnic groups.*

Two leading Singapore architects, William Lim Siew Wai and Tay Kheng Soon, are passionate advocates of low-rise housing, arguing that it not only creates a better life-style, but is cheaper to build than high-rise.

William Lim has written some of the finest and most

comprehensive studies of Singapore's problems in housing and urban development. A staunch patriot and an admirer of much that the Government has done, he is a firm internationalist. Although Singapore is unique, some of its problems may be universal, and William Lim tackles high-rise housing on that basis.

The official reason given to justify the construction of tall buildings for public housing is that land is scarce. Various studies have clearly shown, however, that four-storey housing of appropriate standards can be designed to a residential gross density of 150 to 200 persons per acre (330 to 440 persons per hectare). In the context of a comprehensive land policy, all public housing estates can have option of low-rise buildings. Tall apartment buildings are more expensive to construct and require a longer period of time to build. More skilled workmen and a higher level of building technology are also required. Equipment such as lifts has to be imported and more structural building materials are needed. There are also serious reservations concerning the long-term social and psychological effects on families living in tall buildings. Aware of the disadvantages involved, London has recently decided to stop the construction of tall buildings for public housing.

Certainly, although Singapore is a tiny island and therefore short of land, the visitor cannot help wondering whether better use of land might not be achieved in relation to housing. No one could say, for instance, that there is a shortage of land around the northern centre of the island where the Causeway crosses over from Johore. Yet Woodlands New Town has gone up, tower after tower, across the bare earth, looking just like Ang Mo Kio or Toa Payoh New Towns. But perhaps Woodlands is planned in part to give that high-rise gloss of modernity as the first sight of the nation of Singapore to anyone crossing the Causeway from Peninsular Malaysia.

If this were true, it would have its deeper reasons, for the high-rise is symbolic of the Singapore attitude to life. Clear away the untidy, unsanitary past, put the technocrats in charge, bring in the machines and products of industrialization, be orderly and available for Government inspection, and above all, be educated: without education you can build a *kampong* but without education you could not even pour the foundations of a high-rise. And yet there is ancient knowledge and wisdom behind the building of a *kampong*, whereas education only for technology can stop still in steel and concrete.

The pressures of education in Singapore are extraordinary. Even a French student going for his *Baccalaureat* does not work harder than Singapore students, and the most ambitious of French parents do not push their children harder than Singapore parents. The reasons are there in front of you: from Sago Lane to high-rise; from a one-room flat in an old block due for demolition to a five-room flat in one of the new towns. Time and again Riaz Hassan's interviewers are told that the parents will remain in lowly jobs, but the children, ah, the children may do anything, they may end up as Minister or Head of the H.D.B.

At its best this attitude to the young is admirable, and indeed goes back to Confucius. *The Master said, 'It is fitting that we should hold the young in awe. How do we know that the generations to come will not be the equal of the present? Only when a man reaches the age of 40 or 50 without distinguishing himself in any way can one say, I suppose, that he does not deserve to be held in awe.'* The long view of this sentiment is one that Singapore's leaders might well take to heart, for they are always in such a hurry, whereas education and human development go at a different pace in different individuals. What lovely patience, of Confucius, in giving a man 40 or 50 years to prove himself!

In no other country are the successes of children at school the subject of so many television, radio and newspaper interviews, and in no other country outside the Communist orbit is a classless élite so carefully streamed towards academic success.

Dr. Goh Keng Swee, one of the most remarkable of Singapore's remarkable leaders, was put in charge of Singapore education. His report is now the Bible of education, somewhat to the alarm of the more thoughtful professional educators, for it is a report put together by systems experts from the Ministry of Defence, the oldest of whom was about 28. The Goh Report recommends streaming of children from third year in Primary School; this is carrying élitism about as far as it could go.

Light and shade

Parasol and pick-up

109

One of the most striking features of Lee Kuan Yew's rule in Singapore has been embodied in his Government's constant efforts to anticipate the future, so that planning would be one jump ahead of events. This, of course, presumes a logic and reasonableness in the development of human history which is not borne out by the witness of the past; but once again, Singapore is a special case, where planning has certainly worked up until now. So, 13 years ago Dr. Goh was giving a speech at the Anglo-Chinese School's 81st Founders' Day reunion dinner, saying that Singapore's desperate need for a quantity of education must now grow into a demand for quality of education.

Most surprisingly, in view of the present pressures in Singapore education, Dr. Goh was attacking a system where *there has been far too much emphasis on academic performance. I think this obsession with getting outstanding results in the Cambridge examinations was a very bad thing. After all, much of what a boy or girl learns in school – history, geography, maths or chemistry – will be forgotten in 10 years' time. What is the point, therefore, of all this effort? The real purpose is to distinguish the bright and clever boys and girls from the less bright and clever . . . The preoccupation in Singapore with exam results is unnatural and unhealthy, and we should bring it to an end as early as possible.* The aspects of education which Dr. Goh considered as being neglected in Singapore were: *1) creative imagination, 2) character, 3) moral values . . . Without a widely accepted code of moral values, Singapore will remain what it is now – a community which is basically self-centred and selfish.*

Admirable sentiments for 1967. But the *Straits Times* for 8 March 1980 has headlines and photos devoted to students who *have bagged four A's in the G.C.E. 'A' level examinations*. The success of the top boy at Raffles Institution *brought double happiness to his clerk father and family, for on Tuesday, his younger brother, Chung Yin, had scored eight A.1's in the 'O' level examination. Plus ça change*, one might say, if anyone were learning French in Singapore.

But the comments of some of those same students, interviewed on radio, were very interesting. The interviewer asked them, now they were in the science stream with their five A.1's, what they were going to do. An Indian and a Chinese boy both said they did not know. Another boy, from Raffles Institution, said he did not want to be pinned down yet for the next 70 years. On being asked his recipe for success, he said he had only one message to give students: *Confidence*. He had always done very badly at English, and yet he got an A.1 at the exam.

Wherever you are in Singapore the subject soon gets around to education. At dinner a very attractive young Indian lady, a lawyer, says, with a fetchingly apologetic giggle, that for 10 years she got up at 3 a.m. every morning to do her homework, with her father watching.

A highly intellectual Chinese couple say that their child came home from school with a 90 per cent average. They were in the middle of congratulating him when the phone rang. The boy's form-master was calling to ask whether there were any problems in the boy's life at home. He would have to do better at school. Forty-five per cent of the class had got over 90 per cent.

Parents seek every means to help drive their children on. *Grow*, a Government-sponsored magazine about education, began recently with excellent sales; it now has over 80,000 (S)$10 subscriptions, with trade sales to follow, and is advertised on the back of buses. Where else in the world would such a thing happen?

But those at the top, like Dr. Goh, are conscious of the dangers of these pressures. The general manager of one of the biggest Government enterprises says in private that he was lucky to have been educated at a moderate pace in a not very distinguished school, rather than one of the top schools where competition has always been so fierce.

Choo Hoey, conductor of the Singapore Symphony Orchestra, says it is very difficult to do anything about establishing a youth orchestra because music has been taken off the school syllabus; in the achievement race for training technocrats music is of course of no account.

The general manager of another of the major statutory bodies is very outspoken about the need for something more in education than passing exams. It is interesting that he is an old scholar of the Anglo-Chinese School where Dr. Goh made his speech in 1967. His office, and indeed his whole building, is hung with paintings by modern Singapore artists and he is a genuinely cultivated man.

We need *the arts, and the creative imagination*, he says. *Otherwise we will just be a bunch of hustlers like Hong Kong.* His boys have gone to a Chinese school, and superficially their progress was admirable. But they depressed him, they were so quiet and obedient and good, never up to any mischief, always agreeing with what their parents said. Now after two years of Anglo-Chinese School *they are real tigers, I'll talk to them and they'll answer back, we can discuss things*. This experience confirms the fact, he adds, that the Chinese schools were natural targets for the Communists. He believes strongly in the benefits of the religious instruction at A.C.S., and in the school spirit that has raised millions for buildings, swimming pools and equipment.

The danger of such school spirit in an egalitarian society is that it may not only breed an intellectual but also a social élite. Early in March, 1980, Dr. Tony Tan, then Senior Minister of State for Education, made headlines in the *Sunday Nation*. *The little horrors of A.C.S.: Tony Tan*, read the headline. What he had said was that the Anglo-Chinese School had acquired a reputation for being a school of snobs. (He admitted that he had two sons studying there.) He said there were reports of children asking their parents to drop them some distance from the school because they were ashamed of being seen in their fathers' old cars. *A few parents*, said Dr. Tan, *had even objected to having their children take part in the school's Use Your Hands Campaign. The parents had said they would send their servants to help in the campaign instead*. Dr. Tan slightly softened his blows at the end by saying that it would be wrong to blame the school for the prevalence of such snobbery, *which is a social disease in Singapore associated with the rise of an affluent society*.

Dr. Tan's speech (which was delivered at the A.C. Junior College) was like dumping a load of garbage in the middle of Shenton Way. Two hundred and sixty *A.C.S.ians and friends* signed a letter to the *Straits Times* contending that the school had been *made a scapegoat for a common ailment in the modern Singapore society. Let the people of Singapore examine themselves*. The four Principals of the schools wrote to say that they had been teaching their pupils *the A.C.S. spirit of humility, and service to God and man*. They referred to the *action of some foolish students, out of a total A.C.S. population of 700*.

'Brightness is all'

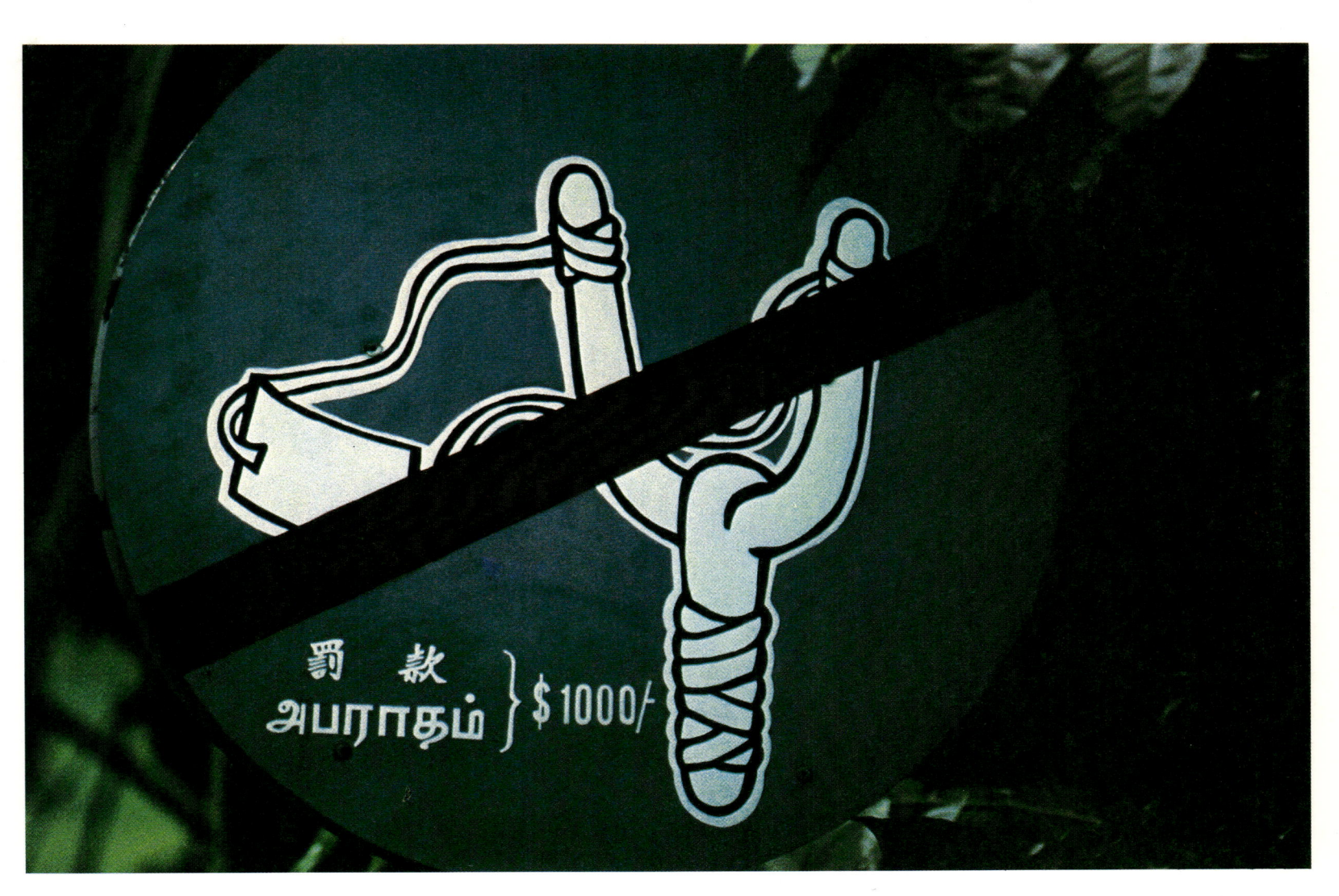

'Thou Shalt Not . . .'

113

The truth, no doubt, is that the children are like the parents. Snobbery is a disease of the newly rich; neither aristocrats nor the poor need to boast. At a lunch party a rich Indian woman says, *I haven't been able to get out of the house for days.* Someone asks what has been wrong. *My chauffeur has been away sick.* After the lunch party someone who has driven in her own car walks down the drive to it. A Chinese lady, amongst those waiting on the steps, calls out: *Ask our chauffeurs to come for us, please.* Their Mercedes and Rolls Royces are fully 50 metres away.

This is all a long way from the *justified arrogance* that the Chinese businessman talked about at the Chinese New Year party. If the snobbery exists at A.C.S. and other schools, it is not nearly as important as independence of spirit and ability to answer back in an argument.

A university lecturer wishes that her students would answer back. When she asks them questions about basic principles they say, *Please, what do you think?* In a recent discussion with her students several of them said, *You must trust politicians.* On one occasion she had been asked to address a group of young people. At the end one of them criticized her for not criticizing Lee Kuan Yew. She said if she had attacked him they would have attacked her. They laughed, and admitted this was true.

Another student said, *You shouldn't have access to too much information.* Whereupon an older student, an ex-policeman, said: *Yes, that's right. You see what has happened in Iran. If they hadn't known about the Shah's excesses, then there wouldn't be this trouble with the hostages.*

She says that students who go overseas often do badly in the Humanities. At school and university they have been trained as technocrats, and they simply do not know how to think. Summing up her years of teaching at the University, she estimates that less than five per cent of students have any independence of mind.

An architect concurs, saying architecture students go to the university merely to *learn the tricks.* He finds in Singapore an extraordinary mixture of enthusiasm and cynicism, based in part on the country's newness. *We Singaporeans are teenagers.* (The People's Action Party won the first general election in 1959.)

He denounces many of the older architects as *bottomless cynics*, men with no artistic feeling whatsoever. Although he strongly opposes high-rise apartment blocks, he says it is not the buildings that cause the many suicides that take place in these blocks. It is simply that with guns being illegal and poisons very difficult to obtain, jumping off buildings is much the most convenient and cheapest way to die. All too frequently in the paper there is a small paragraph headed *Man Falls to Death*. A typical item is: *A 22-year-old man fell to his death from the eighth floor of Block 79, Toa Payoh Central at 2 p.m. yesterday. According to his relatives, he had seemed quite cheerful and had no particular problems.* His problem, says the architect, is that he has failed in the great rat race to succeed.

Education for suicide might be the theme of some of the short stories of Catherine Lim, one of the finest of Singapore's writers in English, whose collection *Little Ironies* has the classic detachment and compassion of a Chekhov or Maupassant. Catherine Lim is herself a teacher.

One of her most powerful stories is called *The Teacher*. It is so condensed and so packed with irony, and says so much about Singapore that it must be quoted in its entirety.

Look, said the teacher to the colleague who was sitting beside him in the staff room. *Look at this composition written by a student in Secondary Four. She's supposed to have had 10 years of studying English, and see what she has written! I'll read it to you. The title of the composition is 'My happiest day'.*

The teacher read, pausing at those parts which he wanted his colleague to take particular note of: *My happiest day it is on that 12 July 1976 I will tell you of that happiest day. My father want me to help him in his cakes stall to sell cakes and earn money. He say I must leave school and stay home and help him. My younger brothers and sisters they are too young to work so they can go to school. My mother is too sick and weak as she just born a baby.* Can anything be more atrocious than this? When she is going to sit for her General Certificate of Education in three months' time! And listen to this:

I was very sad because I don't like to sell cakes I like to learn in school. But I am scare my father he will beat me if I disobeyed him so I cannot say anything to him. He ask me to tell my Principal of my school that I am not going to learn any more. I was scare my Principal will ask me questions. Lucky my mother came home from the hospital where she born the baby, and my mother say to my father that I should learn in school and become nurse later. So I can earn more money. Sell cakes not earn so much money. She begged my father and at last my father agree. I think he agree because he was in good mood. If in bad mood like drunk he will beat my mother up and make trouble in the house. So my mother told me I was no need to stop learning in school. And that was the happiest day in my life which I shall never forget.

The teacher said slowly and meditatively, *I wonder why most of them write like that? Day in, day out, we teach grammar and usage. For my part, I have taught them the use of the Tenses, 'til I'm blue in the face, but they still come up with all kinds of Tense mistakes! I've drummed it into them that when they are writing a story or incident, they have to use the past tense, but I still get hideous mistakes such as the ones you heard just now.*

A week later, the teacher, while correcting composition exercises in the classroom, again dropped his head into his hands in despair. It was a different colleague sitting beside him this time, but the distress in his voice was equally acute as he said, showing her a page from an exercise book: *What do you think of this as a specimen of Secondary Four Composition? I give up! I resign!*

Ah, they are all like that, sighed his colleague in sympathy. *You should see the grammar mistakes I get from my Pre-University students, mind you, Pre-University.*

The teacher held the offending page in front of his colleague, and with his forefinger traced the lines that had given most pain. *Now look at this:*

I would like is become a nurse and successful career so I have a lot of money with luxuries, by the way, I have got them to write on *My Ambition* – so *I can buy a house for my mother and brothers and sisters*. This is the only sentence in the whole composition that is correct grammatically. Listen to this one, can you make anything of it? *And my favourite ambition I must strive very hard and make hard afford for if I have no ambition to help my mother and brothers*

A dying street

A living mosque

and sisters they is sure to suffer for my father he don't care at all every time come back from selling cakes only he must drink and spend all money on drink and sometimes he beats my mother. It's that Tan Geok Peng from Secondary Four C, you know that timid, mousy-looking girl who looks ready to faint in fright the moment you call her to answer a question. You know, I am getting very worried about the standard of English in my class. I guess I shall have to get Tan Geok Peng and the likes of her in for extra Saturday coaching, otherwise they will never make it in the exams. Three months away, I tell them. Just three months in which to polish up your grammar and vocabulary and punctuation, and write the first decent composition in your life!

The extra coaching did not save the poor teacher from the despair he was continually experiencing. *Ah!* he said, shaking his head sadly. *What shall I do? Read this muck! Let me see — yes, it's from that girl, Tan Geok Peng again — that girl will be the death of me, I tell you. I keep explaining things and going over and over the same things with her, but she insists on giving me such nonsense. Listen to this! She was supposed to write a story with the title 'The Stranger' and all she did was write a great deal of trash about her father — 'He canned me everytime, even when I did not do wrong things still he canned me' — She means 'caned' of course — 'And he beat my mother and even if she sick, he wallop her.' This composition was not only grossly ungrammatical but out of point. I had no alternative but to give her an F.9 straight away. God, I wish I could help her!*

When the news reached the school, the teacher was very upset and said, *Poor girl. What? She actually jumped down from the 11th floor? Such a shy, timid girl. If only she had told me of her problems. She was always too shy and timid to speak up.*

The strain of course does not stop at school. The classless society of Singapore is divided into rich, not-so-rich and poor; into those who succeed, those who muddle along and those who fail. Everyone is in a hurry, especially the leaders, so anyone who has trouble finding himself feels an outcast.

* * *

Singapore writers in English have a clear eye for the realities of Singapore. There is a range and depth to their criticism of the quality of life in Singapore, essential achievements for the work of any creative writer. These qualities make nonsense of the myth so zealously promulgated by some Western intellectuals, that Singapore is a police State. Censorship there may be in Singapore, but not of the variety familiar to anyone who has been to a true police State.

Lee's style of government is to make demands on his fellow citizens. The poet Robert Yeo sums them up rather well in a poem about leaving Singapore to take a temporary job in Bangkok. As he says, he intends to come home *still a Singaporean.*

*But O the demands you make
on us Singaporeans!
Since you didn't choose us
but we chose you
(most of us, at any rate
and we still have that choice)
your demands shall be commands.
They shall be observed:
the schools' daily litany
five mornings saluting
five stars and a crescent;
our young men shall bear arms
to deter unnamed enemies;
we shall accept as treasonable
strikes not in the national interest;
south-east Asia's cleanest city
shall be Asia's cleanest city;
we shall enlarge the airport
for the Jumbos
and develop Sentosa
but only for the tourists;
our already low birth-rate
shall further decline;*

*the world's fourth largest port
shall become the world's third largest port;
we shall keep our hair short,
we shall continue to view Art
as an adjunct to Culture
serving Politics.*

The demands of Singapore are far-reaching: discipline, self-reform, ambition, energy, the children studying in the high-rise flats, the limitation of the family to two children. A Malay newspaper editor who already has two children says he longs for a third and he feels a hypocrite when he writes editorials reminding Singaporeans of the wisdom of the Government's policy to restrict families to two. In fact, one of the unarguable miracles of Singapore has been the success of family planning amongst people of three races, for each of whom a large number of children has been traditionally prestigious. Lee Kuan Yew himself has three children: but they were born in the 1950's.

Lee says that in his makeup there is *a thick layer of Confucian discipline, which I believe in as a method of preventing our society from just being a cheap imitation of the West.* This discipline is a two-way business, as Confucius himself pointed out. *Chi K'ang Tzu asked Confucius about government. Confucius answered, 'To govern* (cheng) *is to correct* (cheng)*'. 'If you set an example by being correct, who would dare to remain incorrect?'* The translator, D.C. Lau, points out, with reference to the word 'cheng', *besides being homophones, the two words in Chinese are cognate, thus showing that the concept of 'governing' is felt to be related to that of 'correcting'.*

What is perennially attractive about Singaporeans is their capacity, whatever their race, education or economic status, to think responsibly about other people. However much they may be taken to task by their own people for being materialistic, or snobs, or selfish, their pride in being Singaporeans still brings that precious gift, becoming so rare in the world today, of believing that some good may come from their efforts, that all is not lost in corruption, chicanery and venality. Singapore cannot afford cynicism, the luxury of the secure. It gives its people hope of being, although a small nation, not a nation of small men. Confucius would have seen hope in them, for in the saying that precedes the answer to Chi K'ang Tzu about government, *The Master said 'The gentleman helps others to realize what is good in them; he does not help them to realize what is bad in them. The small man does the opposite.'*

Chopsticks: (1)

Chopsticks: (2)

"This image of themselves"

One of the accidental jokes of the world, that has entertained thousands of innocent travellers, is that the tag the airline puts on your baggage when you go to Singapore is labelled SIN. The label is deliciously inappropriate, as is a notice to be seen in front of a building in Chinatown, 'SIN CONFERENCE HALL.' Appropriately enough, it is not far from the premises of the MORAL UPLIFT SOCIETY. Singapore's morals are cleaned up regularly, and although of course there are whores and gambling, and Bugis Street wriggles its transvestite buttocks, you just don't go to Singapore for the sort of 'good time' you find in Las Vegas or Rio de Janeiro or even Bangkok. Hunter Thompson's brilliant book *Fear and Loathing in Las Vegas* is about a real Sin City. Paul Theroux's mild, sad and entertaining *Saint Jack*, although about a pimp in Singapore, conveys nothing of an environment of vice. It is ironic that the Singapore authorities should indignantly have banned the film of the book, which shows a completely fictional Singapore rich in vice, for if they were allowed to view the film, Singaporeans might well relax in a glow of conscious virtue.

The Seven Deadly Sins, without which life would not be tolerable anywhere, do have their place in Singapore. The most readily available, happily enough, must surely be gluttony. There may be greater restaurants in Paris, but of all cities in the world Singapore is the one which offers, at every level of cost and comfort, the most sumptuous variety of meals. There are gaps in the national cuisines to be sampled – Southern Indian, for instance – but in Singapore you can dine wonderfully well on Chinese, Indian, Malay and European food. And, of course, there is that superb mixture of cuisines which is Singapore food, although the true Nonya dishes of Straits Chinese cooking can only be truly tasted in private houses.

Even in France there are simple, cheap restaurants, but no other city can surpass the vigour and satisfaction of the Singapore hawkers' stalls. They used to be scattered around and are now more concentrated, but the quality is as good as ever.

Singapore is proud of its freedom from class distinctions. This is particularly true of its restaurants – Chinese, Malay, Indian or European. There is no more democratic eating place in the world than a Singapore hawker's stall or a sea-food restaurant on the coast.

Take the hawker's stall in Armenian Street, not far from Coleman's beautiful little Armenian church. Singaporeans eat at all hours of the day, and they love to eat out. It is almost impossible to find a seat in this stall from 11 a.m. to 2 p.m. People come to a place like this to eat. Talking goes on, but is of secondary importance. Sitting and dreaming and twirling a glass and looking at your beloved in silence is unthinkable. Here you have the dapper executive in his Gucci shoes and his Pierre Cardin shirt; two housewives with their children; a group of young clerks yelling jovially at each other across their beer mugs; a grave old man who might be a street sweeper; an English family group; four pretty secretaries from the nearby office; and through them, weaving, a man who you couldn't really call a waiter, bearing tea or beer or lemonade, swishing a cloth first over the zinc-topped table before setting down his burden. There is no outside or inside to this eating place, there are no doors or windows, and the pedestrians and motorists can sniff the food cooking on the edge of the footpath as they go past. There are no menus.

On the main street front a big fellow with a boxer's bent face specializes in sausages and fish-balls and beancurd. You just select what you want and he fries and anoints it, and while it is cooking he takes up his huge cleaver, and swishing it up and down so fast you can hardly see it, he dismembers a cucumber or an onion or a water chestnut – bang! bang! bang! bang! – and there are the slim slices falling with never a finger lost. At the next stall to his there is a more solemn, skinny man, cooking chicken and rice and sliced smoked pork. Facing the side street, on the other side, is a tiny little man dancing in front of the coals of his brazier stirring noodles in a huge *kuali*, or *wok*, throwing in eggs, soya sauce, oil and other sauces and then tossing an egg-slice load of noodles on to a plate, flicking the odd droopy noodle back into the centre of the *wok*. Two beers and a chicken, pork and rice dish for two costs (S)$7.20, (S)$4 for the beer and (S)$3.20 for the food. If you want to eat in a hurry, these cooks put Western 'fast food' in the shade. It's all cooked and on your plate long before a hamburger or fish and chips would be ready. (Alas, however, there are beach-heads of those harbingers of culinary doom, McDonald's and Colonel Sanders, already established in Singapore, the specious glamour of the foreign drawing some Singaporeans into them alongside the tourists who insistently stick to the familiar.)

Or take Chin Lee's Sea Foods at Tuas in Jurong, due for demolition as the new port is developed, and in the meantime looking like a survivor of a bomb raid. Mercedes and Volvos are parked three-deep around the debris, and diners sit at tables on the wooden floor above the stilts going down into mud or water, depending on the tide. The eating habits here are long and slow, businessmen of all races from the Jurong factories and offices taking their time, a group of soldiers drinking lots of Chinese beer, two families each with four little children (who have either been defying Singapore's family planning exhortations to stop at two, or who have borrowed another pair each for the day).

The waitresses in this indescribably cheerful, haphazard, dilapidated setting bring dish after marvellous dish from the huge braziers that look as if they might burn down the whole flimsy wooden structure: a whole *garupa* nestling in oysters and coriander leaves and ginger; little grilled crabs; the tails of fiery prawns with their shells still on, mixed with dried red chillies; softer, big peeled prawns in a sweet-sour sauce; prawn rolls so crisp that when you bite them they seem to have been held together by nothing more than their aroma; tiny whole crackling squid. All the ingredients taste as if they had just come out of the sea, as indeed they have, the Jurong fish market being close by, and there are in fact fresh green prawns and fresh crawling lobsters available for sale in a shed outside the restaurant.

In all the simple Singapore stalls and restaurants (simple in their settings, that is, not in the subtleties of their cooking), there is a sense of participating in the actual cooking, the frenzy of stirring and chopping and dashing for more ingredients, as it all takes place in front of you. What is *not* present, amazingly enough to anyone who has eaten out in the tropics, is the usual crowd of unwelcome fellow-diners, cockroaches, flies and rats. Inspectors pounce on restaurants and a fine is imposed if cockroaches are found, but the amount raised must be miniscule. Even in the big

Old man, Bugis Street

Young man, Bugis Street

125

open areas of hawkers' stalls such as Newton Circus, there are no cockroaches, let alone rats. As for flies, a letter to the *Straits Times*, early in 1980, gives an idea of the seriousness with which Singaporeans take these matters. FLIES MAKE AN UNWELCOME REAPPEARANCE. *Recently with members of my family, we had the occasion of eating out at a coffee house along Orchard Road, the Hawker's Centre next to the Capital Cinema.*

One unbelievable common feature that struck us at all these four places was the presence of flies flying around our tables — something we have not seen in Singapore for some good many years.

It was rather disturbing to us then (while eating) to think that the Keep Singapore Clean Campaign being over, our standard of cleanliness had deteriorated that rapidly.

However, the report in the Sunday Times *of Nov. 25 that a mild case of cholera was confirmed in Singapore suggests the seriousness of our observations of flies at these public eating places.*

It has been reported that an epidemiological investigation is in progress to trace the source of infection.

However, apart from normal health considerations, a place like Singapore, with the economy also cashing in on the tourist industry, cannot afford to have epidemics of any nature and the standard of cleanliness in public eating places, lavatories, etc., must of necessity be very high at all times.

One of the most famous of Singapore eating places is Fatty's in Albert Street, still unspoiled, despite its fame. Most of the street and all the footpath are taken up with people eating at tables, and the cooks lunging and sluicing and stirring in huge *woks*, ladling out great plates of prawns and crabs and ducks and whole fish. If there is no room left downstairs, as often there is not, you go upstairs. Maybe you fancy the table by the window, which has just been vacated, with heaps of crockery and cutlery still on it. A waitress with a build like a wrestler and a nose the shape of a burglar's jemmy shows you to another table. *That one too hot, nicer here.* A few minutes later a big Chinese family arrives and she takes them to the table by the window, now nicely cleaned up. *Not too hot for them?* someone calls out. She roars with laughter and barks, like a dog rounding up a stray sheep, at a man carrying dishes, who shouts back at her. Whoever said that the Chinese were a quiet, discreet people? The whole restaurant bangs and shakes most jovially throughout the evening. The clientele is international, a Sikh and his family at a corner table, two young Australians next to them. An American and a New Zealander and an Australian are choosing their dinner, ordering by numbers off the menu while the waitress looks around the room, taking no notice. *I guess we'll get what we're given*, says the American.

But all six dishes arrive exactly as ordered, plus huge mugs of beer. The food is delicious, straightforward as the place itself, a huge steamed pomfret, sweet and sour prawns, beef and dark-red chilies, chicken in oyster sauce, duck with cashews and chestnuts, rice. There is no fancy décor or soft music, just battered green tiles on the floor, heaps of beer bottles against the wall, a little sky through the barred window, a well-clothed Chinese girl on a wall calendar, and the overhead fans belting out a heavy breeze. Outside, across the street, a handsome girl stands at an open window leaning out by a curtain. The food and fruit stalls are doing good business. A surge of tourists goes through, followed by a dozen trishaws. But at Fatty's no one is distracted from eating, cooking, and handing the food and drink around, making jokes with the guests.

Eat as much as you can, it still does not seem like gluttony, let alone a sin, even in the much more classically simple surroundings of one of Singapore's superlative Indian restaurants, like the Rang Mahal or the Omar Khayyam. There is an excellent *sitar* player from India with accompanying musicians, the waiters glide and speak softly, lovers are quiet in a corner, there are wines available (at ferocious prices, like all wines in Singapore).

But there is no drunkenness, which in medieval days was included in the sin of gluttony. Once again, you can find sinners in Singapore, drunks who are mostly Americans or Australians, but the Singaporeans themselves do not drink much, although the Chinese have an occasional blow-out on brandy. Singapore beer would not make anyone drunk; it is simply a way of keeping the pores open in the tropics.

If the sin of gluttony is available everywhere in Singapore, the sin of lechery is almost invisible. In this respect Singapore's rulers are as solicitous for the morals of the people as are the Communists. *Playboy* and *Penthouse* and such magazines are banned, blue movies are not to be seen, girls dress modestly, and although bikinis exist on the beaches, skinny-dipping does not. Teenagers can still be innocent in Singapore, a happy phenomenon sadly rare in the world today. The mood is deftly caught in a poem by Robert Yeo.

Mummy what shall I wear?
The blue mini
shall I wear that blue skirt
the one you made for me

How shall I look tonight?
This is my third date
with him, and the last time
he said I just looked great

Mummy may I use your lipstick?
Not the Christian Dior
I prefer the Max Factor one
the one you caught daddy dear

He's taking me tonight, mummy,
to the Rasa Sayang
and how shall I dance tonight?
What's the meaning of rasa sayang?

And if he wants to hold me close
tonight as he did last week
shall I let him, mummy, please?
May I dance cheek to cheek?

And if he wants to kiss me
mummy, shall I let him?
I don't know when to close my eyes
will it all seem like a dream?

Love: Tiger Balm Gardens

Marriage: Indian bride

It is a nice touch that the girl does not even know what Rasa Sayang means. (It is a Malay phrase which roughly translated means *a love for life*.)

But of course Singapore is no innocent teen-age city. Evidence of depravity surfaces rather entertainingly from time to time, such as in the information in the newspaper that a certain bar has been refused a renewal of its licence because it is 'a haunt of prostitutes and catamites'. One might be pardoned for reaching for one's dictionary to find out that a catamite is 'a boy kept for unnatural purposes'. One recalls the early history of the sexual imbalance in Singapore.

Paul Theroux's Saint Jack is a genial pimp who does his bit to help out over this question of the imbalance, though strictly no catamites for him. His sinful friends and clients are monuments to human lechery, for the book is really about the past, not about Singapore as it is now. Though rapes are reported in the newspapers, and girls are molested in high-rise lifts, the modern Singaporean's official attitude to lust is perfectly summed up in an item in the *Straits Times* early in 1980.

SIX MONTHS JAIL FOR MOLESTING GIRL AT EXPO

A factory supervisor who molested a fourteen year old student, was caught by the girl's elder brother.

In a Magistrate's Court yesterday . . . [a] supervisor with an engineering company in Lavender Street, admitted the offence and was jailed for six months.

The girl, with her mother and three brothers, were at the Sims Avenue Exposition in New Sims Avenue, on Sunday when [he] approached her, pressed her left breast and walked away. She screamed and one of her brothers chased and caught [him] at the entrance.

One wonders what the scale of retribution must be, whether there is a mathematical progression based on the original equation of: squeeze of left breast equals six months.

Singapore is enclosed by a moat of morality, over which the Causeway is in effect more like a drawbridge, allowing the wicked out but not in. Lust and its attendant pornography, violence and sexual aberration are effectively classed as something foreign, a mood sardonically caught in a poem by Arthur Yap.

twin-point

but that is not the point:

it is well executed
this foreign woman, painted
roughly to look violated
(so it means) you know what
you can do with her

so she has been pummelled
and much battered, an angry red x
added on her spread of thighs
so it means (afterwards)
she is colourfully censored.

the point is the painter's anger
has only killed a foreign woman . . .

Not long ago a German psychologist announced that his researches had convinced him that envy was the deadliest sin of the Western world. Singapore is of course not Western, despite the veneer of industrial and technological activity. There are certainly rich and poor in Singapore, there are the Western pressures for people to be conspicuous consumers and get on and up in life, and ferocious pressures in education, but the bitter rancour of envy does not seem to have blighted Singapore.

The self-made man is happy with his Mercedes and his handmade furniture, and no one else seems to wish him anything but the best of luck. He will take you happily to the big new shopping centre where he has four sections, (S)$1.5 million worth, for his shops, and will show you every gadget, each of which he knows by name. He came from Canton 32 years ago with £100 and his tough little face crinkles around his flat nose with the memory of all the hard work and the joy of success. He has a lovely wife, but one of the children is a problem, idle, does not want to work. He shows you into his house and tells you immediately that it is 7,000 square metres. He has all the Western drinks in his cocktail cabinet and mixes them with alarming generosity, but drinks only tea himself. The rosewood furniture is all new, the wood is from Thailand, and has been made by craftsmen in Singapore. He was in Europe in January and will be in Australia in July. The only thing wrong with Singapore is the climate; he comes from Canton where there are four seasons, and although he starts the day in the cool at 6 a.m. he gets tired. His shops are open from 10 in the morning until 9.30 at night. *Singapore is the best place!* he says. And who would doubt him?

A visiting Englishman says, '*Lee Kuan Yew should be loaned out for periods to various countries around the world, starting with England*'. '*Maybe in a big country like England Lee wouldn't work*', muses the man from Canton. '*Here, very small, we put up with being told some of the things we are not to do. But Singapore is still the best place!*'

He does not envy those who live in even more square feet and have a second Mercedes for the wife (his has a Datsun). Perhaps he suffers from the sin of covetousness?

Covetousness and envy are inseparable in the West where millions and millions of human donkeys are led on by the carrots of advertising and pushed forward by the goads of Union demands. The Unions, which were originally formed to secure justice for the workers, and sometimes still do, have in many countries become the expression of organized envy. The man of talent who works hard and makes a fortune is admired by the workers in the U.S.A., for the tradition of the country is that success will take you to the top, no matter how humbly you began. In England the class system still counts for so much that those below are reduced to taking a wry satisfaction in levelling down those above. In Australia the instinctive democracy of the people is haunted by a hatred and suspicion, dating back to the country's convict origins, of those on top.

Singapore is perhaps unique in the world in its ability to keep

Martial arts

Martial music

sin and covetousness apart, and, even more remarkable, keep them private, sins of the individual rather than the masses. The leaders of Singapore must be given a lot of the credit for this. Both in their private life-styles and in their public pronouncements they have succeeded in convincing Singaporeans that it is not worth wrecking the State for private pleasures, and that a certain modesty is becoming. When the self-made man says, *Singapore is the best place*, he does not only mean the best place in which to make money. Lee Kuan Yew himself put it very well when he said: *From a riotous, volatile, unstable, unpredictable society, we have become stable and predictable, politically and economically. All this was brought about because there was a hard core of people who, for a number of reasons, put cause before self.*

It is instructive to speak to C. V. Devan Nair, President of the Singapore National Trades Union Congress, a man frequently vilified by Marxists for making Trade Unions a tool of Government policy. (These same critics are always seemingly unaware that this is exactly what Trade Unions are in Communist countries.) Devan Nair was one of the seven top Trade Union leaders arrested and jailed in 1956 by the British Colonial Authorities. He decided in jail that the real battle for Singapore was not going to be fought against the British, who were going to give in anyway, but against the Communists who wanted to dominate an independent Singapore. He was also deeply distrustful of the Communists for their Chinese chauvinism, which would be disastrous in multi-racial Singapore.

The old brigade of Singapore's leaders, Lee Kuan Yew, Goh Keng Swee, S. Rajaratnan and C. V. Devan Nair all have a finely uninhibited ability to state their case in non-bureaucratic language. Devan Nair can be left to describe himself, the non-envious, non-covetous character of Trade Unions in Singapore.

We are aware that we enjoy a status, prestige and influence in the public life of the nation, which is the envy of other Trade Unions in other developing countries. This has been achieved by dint of the fact that we were in part of a wider scope and an ampler sweep, to our objectives as a Trade Union movement in a developing society. While collective bargaining remains our primary responsibility to the workers of

Singapore, it has ceased to be the sole or exclusive concern of our Trade Unions.

Visitors to Singapore have often been struck, and have said so publicly, by the palpable sense of pride among our workers and the fact that one in every three life insurance policies sold in Singapore is an NTUC income policy: that about 1600 owner-driver taxis bearing the insignia of the NTUC travel our roads day and night; that four (soon to be eight) supermarkets, co-operatively owned and managed by the NTUC and its affiliate Unions, play a crucial role in combating the profiteering by certain groups of the private sector; that the Trade Union Movement founded and launched CASE – The Consumer Association of Singapore – which has effectively taken up the grievances of hundreds of Singapore consumers given a raw deal by retailers of various kinds of merchandise; that thousands of schoolchildren in several Singapore schools and their parents have benefitted from the operations of the NTUC's School Textbooks Co-operative, Fair-Deal; and that even more projects by the NTUC and some of its affiliate Unions are in the pipeline . . .

The truth is that Singapore labour enjoys, next to Japan, the highest income levels in Asia. This is a cause for worry, and not for elation. The problem is to curb wage increases in Singapore, so that our wages are not excessively high in comparison with wage levels in countries like South Korea, Taiwan and Hong Kong. The chances are that if we fail to regulate our wage increases, the goods that we manufacture in Singapore may well be priced out of the world market.

Lee Kuan Yew has also been quoted as saying that he stands for an elitist society. This is again a gross misrepresentation. The truth is that class conflicts in Singapore are much less acute than they are in Great Britain, for example. This is ensured by our education system. There are no special schools for the privileged. No matter what the social and economic class of the parents may be, people of all classes in society are obliged to send their children to the same school. The result is that many members of the professional and executive elite in Singapore are the offspring of the washerwomen and street hawkers of yesteryear. We have thereby ensured, in Singapore, a very high degree of social mobility.

One of the most interesting aspects of Devan Nair's own character is his concern for basic ideals as well as pragmatic morals. His opening remarks in an essay on trade unions in Singapore are worth quoting.

There is a fundamental fallacy in judging the Third World on the basis of the standards, values and achievements of the advanced industrial nations of the West. In the first place, all value judgements, in so far as they relate to the political and socio-economic conditions and circumstances, are relative, and therefore likely to be biased and one-sided. If at all there are seminal values, they belong not to the realm of politics, economics and sociology. They belong, rather, to the non-mundane spheres covered by the great spiritual mentors of mankind, figures like Christ and Buddha, who speak not of relative values, but of fundamental and universally applicable values of goodness, beauty, truthfulness and selflessness. Christ from his cross did more to humanise Europe than all the politicians, ideologists, churchmen and system-builders put together. And the gentle voice of the Buddha, echoing down the centuries, has influenced individual human behaviour all over Asia infinitely more than the entire glittering galaxy of emperors and warlords, sultans and maharajas, pundits and mandarins, taken together.

So it is instructive to talk to him at a time when one of his own protégés, Phey Yew Kok, holding no less a position than that of Chairman of the NTUC, has skipped bail on charges of criminal breach of trust of a total of (S)$82,520, using as his escape money the (S)$10,000 raised by his supporters for his defence. Sitting at his desk in his office, which is more like that of an art gallery director than a Trade Union leader, Devan Nair sadly waves to a pile of papers on his desk and admits to having to restructure two of his biggest Unions. *He fooled me,* he says, *one of my own protégés. He still had his passport, as an MP, and he used it to fly to Kuala Lumpur and then Bangkok. You can buy any passport, or anything else, there. Now he will be in South America. It is so bad for the image of the Unions.* He is slightly comforted by Lee Kuan Yew saying to him, *Don't worry if one of your protégés has turned out bad, think of all the good ones.*

He is not happy with the state of British Unions but he very much admires British *decency*, which may be in peril. He is an admirer of the Australian Nobel Prize-winner Patrick White, and can talk in depth about his novels. He is obviously a man who cares deeply for what he calls *seminal values.*

But he is still the leader of a Trade Union movement that has

National Day: The Prime Minister...

... *The President*

been hit twice in one week by corruption. After Phey Yew Kok's defection there was the trial of Irene Yeo Chooi Lan, the first woman to be elected a vice-chairman of the NTUC, who was fined (S)$4,500 or three charges of forging rebate vouchers. The prosecution proceeded on only three of the 132 charges against her, so it seems she was lucky to have got off with a (S)$4,500 fine. She wept in the dock when she pleaded guilty. Her defence was ingenious. She was working under Phey Yew Kok in running the Trade Union Co-operative supermarket, and said that there was no dialogue between him and the committees and the employees. When she complained about anything she was told not to be negative, a phrase very much part of his vocabulary. So she forged the rebate vouchers, *To shock him into realisation that even his trusted aides could abuse their position*. Perhaps, if he had not flitted from Singapore, Phey Yew Kok could have used the same defence in relation to Devan Nair.

These ominous outbreaks of covetousness in leaders who, to reverse Lee Kuan Yew's words, *for a number of reasons, put self before cause*, may be signs of the perils Singapore will have to face as it becomes a more and more affluent society.

Lee Kuan Yew and his old colleagues have long memories and that sense of history which they insist is vital to the understanding of Singapore and to the enduring welfare of Singaporeans. They are also profoundly aware that Singapore's most dangerous hidden sin is anger. When Lee Kuan Yew refers to Singapore's formerly *riotous, volatile, unstable, unpredictable society*, he is looking at anger.

The anger still exists, despite the universal politeness and exemplary self-control of most Singaporeans. It can erupt suddenly, and seriously, an explosion of tamped-down forces, like a pressure-cooker giving way.

Author Dennis Bloodworth, speaking from his deep knowledge of the Chinese character, says that this tendency to sudden explosion is typical of the Chinese. You can live in Singapore for a month and never be the victim of a rude word. Far from it, you can be the recipient of extraordinary politeness. You can lose your way driving at night (easy enough in Singapore's one-way streets) and stop to look at the street map with the aid of the interior light of the car. You look up to see three tough young men approaching, crossing the street and bearing down purposefully on your car. Having been in violent countries, you are about to drive off at high speed when one of the young men calls out, *Please can we help you find your way.* There is earnest discussion amongst the young men, directions are punctiliously given, they wave goodbye and wish you good luck.

Then one peaceful morning you stop at the corner of Napier Road to buy a permit to drive along the Orchard Road restricted zone at 9 a.m. There is a queue of cars double-parked. In front there is a Mercedes, its owner affixing the permit to his windscreen. There is another car to the left, the ticket booth is ahead to the right. Behind, there is a small pick-up truck whose driver is blipping his horn. There is nothing you can do until the man in the Mercedes moves on. Suddenly, hammering at the window is a 25-year-old Chinese, the driver of the truck, tense and furious, screaming: *You bloody hell man. How you park your car?* He shakes his fist. Fortunately the Mercedes drives off, you restrain your indignation and follow him. It is an outburst of the classic anger of a thousand restraints that have become one thousand and one and can no longer be restrained. Perhaps it is the penalty of incessant politeness.

There is another anger, of historical causes. Lee Kuan Yew could well remember that anger erupting in 1950 over what might seem a trivial issue, the decision of the Singapore Colonial Authorities to return a Dutch Eurasian girl, Maria Hertogh, to her mother in Holland. During the Japanese occupation she had lost contact with her parents, who had been interned, and had been brought up by a Muslim family and had married a Muslim. In three days of rioting, which was stirred up by the Malay press, eight Eurasians and Europeans were killed and 173 injured.

The Prime Minister would remember a students' strike in 1956, which led to riots, fire and murder. He would remember the days when Unions fought against Unions, and the multi-racial harmony of Singapore seemed doomed to destruction.

The mood of those times is poignantly fresh in Lloyd Fernando's novel *Scorpion Orchid*. Its four male characters, Indian, Malay, Chinese and English, the young whore Sally, and the mysterious old medium Tok Said, are all torn apart from each other in Singapore's troubles of the 1950's. Sally is raped by unknown men; the four friends fall apart. The violence and anger of the time make them *think for the first time, and ironically, the very first fruits of that thinking had been to set them apart very subtly from one another.* In a moment of desperation, one of them, Sabran, realizes that *they had come apart because they had not really believed.* The Chinese protagonist, Guan Kheng, is convinced that this anger is a legacy of the colonial era.

Had it been foolish after all, to have believed we could make a go of it as one country, he wondered. In the University the ideal seemed alluringly close. Sabran and Santinathan and Peter seemed a microcosm of a presage of a new society, a world of new people who would utterly confound the old European racialist ways of thinking. How did these hopes stand now? There had been an unconscious arrogance, he now realised, in their seeing themselves in the centre of great events. They had been enticed into an ambience which, after all, was local to another place, but only marginal here. Perhaps that was why it was so hard to discover what contribution one could make.

But where was the heart of things? Was it in the mindless violence which now plagued the streets? Surely not. But that it was in a violence of some kind, he was convinced. A soundless fury which confused birth and dying, and left growth to find a new relation to each. That was what they had to understand. That was the true blight of the colonial era. Its invisible presence created goblins which everywhere interfered with the discovery of originality.

Lee Kuan Yew and his colleagues believe that the mindless anger of Singapore can be cured by belief in the new Nation of Singapore. They have certainly done their best to give Singaporeans something to believe in, and the effort has been worth it. Singapore is a community relatively free of the great Western malaise, cynicism.

Cynicism must surely be closely allied to that most subtle of the deadly sins, sloth, or *accidie*, as it was called in Chaucer's day. Once the subject of an excellent essay by Aldous Huxley, it is really more than sloth, or torpor: it is a real sickness of the spirit.

Parade in the rain . . .

... *Parade in the sun*

Singaporeans are assuredly quite free of that sin, not only because of their frenetic activity (they must surely be the most energetic people in the world), but also because of their pride. This of course was for centuries of Christian belief regarded as the deadliest of sins, for it was through pride that Satan fell, and man set himself up to defy God. Though a due humility before the greatest of Gods, the purity of the Way, or the wisdom of the Master, is common to all the religions of all the races of Singapore, modern Singaporeans themselves are united in the sin of pride, believing (and surely not without reason) that it is no sin at all to be proud of one's country. In a way their *justified arrogance*, to use the words of that Singapore businessman, is balanced by discipline, which is a form of humility. They humble themselves not towards Lee Kuan Yew, for he is no dictator, but before the concept of an ordered society to which they all contribute, not only in taxes, military service and the acceptance of certain losses of freedom, but in the belief in something bigger than themselves.

The four young heroes of Lloyd Fernando's novel were broken apart because they did not believe; they had not had time to discover themselves and the possibility of belief. The Singapore that Singaporeans have created in the few years of its independent existence is more than a profit-making business that is doing well, the island of order behind the moat of security, the stainless society with its leaders polishing its image. It is more than its Prime Minister, although a leading Malay Singaporean can say to you without irony, *Lee Kuan Yew is Singapore's only hero*. Singapore is so small, so vulnerable, so teen-age in its development, that people can feel proud of it as they can of a successful child. There is no sin in that.

The founder of the Christian religion, when confronted by a group about to stone a woman taken in adultery, said: *Let him who is without sin cast the first stone*. If one might be allowed to make a pun on a sacred text and substitute the abbreviation SIN for the noun, one could produce a great many examples of foreigners (not all of them Marxists) who have delighted in throwing stones at Singapore. There is a distinctly rancorous virtue about such critics, who invariably are from countries which enjoy established law and order with none of Singapore's potential problems. Perhaps the most famous flash-point for their indignation was Lee Kuan Yew's edict about long hair, epitomized in the unforgettable poster showing a hippie and the legend, *those with long hair will be served last*. That and the death sentence for drug running seem to have aroused as much indignation amongst these critics as the Soviet imprisonment of dissenters.

The real coming test for Lee Kuan Yew and his successors is going to be not in the stones thrown from outside, nor in the discredited Communists, but in the ability or failure of the Singapore Government to allow dissent from within, and the dangers of instability inherent in education. At one stage in Singapore's development it was perfectly justifiable for Lee Kuan Yew to say: *The more we persist in producing men who are educated, but unable to increase productive capacity, the more we are heading for an unstable situation.* Singapore now has a good and increasing supply of technocrats and productive workers, both trained and in training. The development of the distinctive Singapore culture is going to call for educated people whose ability *to increase productive capacity* is of a more subtle nature. Lee Kuan Yew (as usual) is well aware of this, when he says that *one of the most important purposes of all this planning and effort is that, at the end of each day's toil, life should be more than just existence, and the business of making a living. Social objectives which can raise the quality of life must accompany the hard-headed pursuit of economic and security objectives.*

Somehow or another there must be created a distinctive Singapore quality of life. The ingredients are dramatically mixed in the heritages of Chinese, Malay, Indian and English civilizations and languages; and there is an added complication in the need to integrate a rapidly emancipated female population. It is important, in trying to understand and interpret Singapore, to realize that the immense legacy of British rule did not include any contribution from women. The wives of Straits Settlements planters and businessmen were often the very worst type of the British female, spoilt, idle and condescending. They were beautifully described by a lady named Isabella Bird in 1883.

A tall, graceful, kling *woman, draped as I have described, gliding along the pavement, her statuesque figure the perfection of graceful ease, a dark pitcher on her head, just touched by the beautiful hand, showing the finely moulded arm, is a beautiful object, classical and warm, exquisite in movement, and artistic in colouring, the creation of the tropic sun. What thinks she, I wonder, if she thinks at all, of the pale European, paler for want of exercise and engrossing occupation, who steps out of her carriage in front of her, an ungraceful heap of* poufs *and frills, tottering painfully on high heels, in tight boots, her figure distorted into the shape of a Japanese* sake *bottle, every movement a struggle or a jerk, the clothing utterly unsuited to this or any climate, impeding motion, and affecting health, comfort, and beauty alike?*

It is only the European part of Singapore which is dull and sleepy looking. No life and movement congregate around the shops. The merchants, hidden away behind jalousies in their offices, or dashing down the streets in covered buggies, make but a poor show. Their houses are mostly pale, roomy, detached bungalows, almost altogether hidden by the bountiful vegetation of the climate. In these, their wives, growing paler every week, lead half-expiring lives, kept alive by the efforts of the ubiquitous 'punkah-wallahs', writing for the mail, the one active occupation.

The best of the British Singapore women found their activities restricted to good works of a patronizing kind. The redoubtable British ladies of the 19th and early 20th centuries who made such achievements in women's emancipation, science, art and literature, had no counterparts in Singapore or Malaya.

And in the local scene, the only Singapore culture with tradition and coherence, that of the Straits Chinese, the Babas, kept women, the Nonyas, in utter subjection. It was a paradoxical situation, because the Straits Chinese men were intensely pro-British, as had been observed by a visitor, Henry Norman, very early in Singapore's history.

The Straits Chinaman would not exchange his British nationality for anything else in the world; he plays cricket, football, and lawn tennis; he has his annual athletic sports; the recreation ground, and indeed every open space, is covered in the afternoons with Chinese engaged in these games; he goes to the Free Library; and he reads the newspapers; he attends the

Malay wedding pageant

Indian wedding pageant

Debating Society and he carries off prizes at the Raffles' School; he eats foreign food and imitates foreign vices. When he is prosperous he drives through the streets in a carriage and pair with a European coachman on the box. He knows he is the equal of the Englishman before the law, and considers that he is slightly superior to him in other respects. He looks upon the Civil Service as his servants, on the Governor as his ruler, on the Forts as his protection, on the whole place as his home.

But Straits Chinese women were not allowed to share these attitudes. The Singapore Director of Public Construction said in 1906, *There is no more absolutely ignorant, prejudiced and superstitious class of people in the world than the Straits-born Chinese woman.* In 1913 Miss Lee Choo Neo, herself daringly studying at the Straits Medical School, wrote an article for *The Queen* in which she said, *The Chinese girl's life in the Straits Settlements, though freer and less irksome than that of her sister in China, is not an enviable one. Its monotony is intolerable ... she is apparently well contented with her lot, for she makes no complaint whatever ... the life is indeed lonely and dull ... she is never permitted to venture outside the doors of her abode, unless to pay occasional visits to her closest relatives. When she does go out it is in conveyances which are entirely covered up, and either her mother or an aged relative acts as her chaperone. She lives in a sphere of her own, quite out of touch with the society of men ... the Chinese girl is seldom provided with an adequate education, the passing of the third and fourth standards being deemed sufficient ... according to Chinese custom, it is indecent, and disgraceful for girls to work for their living.*

It is astonishing to reflect that this was how Lee Kuan Yew's late mother, Mrs. Lee Chin Koon, grew up, in exactly the environment of the Baba Chinese and the Nonya women. Being a resourceful girl of high spirit, she managed to educate herself to a certain extent with the help of books of a friendly English schoolteacher; otherwise her life was entirely enclosed. Mrs. Lee was a remarkable woman, who wrote books about Nonya cooking, with its highly subtle dishes. She had an excellent memory and talked to me vividly about her early life.

We were known as 'Peranakan' and not 'Chinese.' 'Peranak' means 'born' and 'kan' is 'here.' We were born here, so we speak Malay. Our culture is partly Malay and partly Chinese. In our dress, in our food and in our language, we were Malays.

As young girls, we were not educated, our education was in the home. Our parents wanted to make sure that we were well brought up as we got married young and had to go into our mother-in-law's house. If we were not well brought up, our mothers-in-law sent us back home as an insult to our parents, saying 'you did not train your daughter properly.' Therefore, from morning to night we spent all of our childhood cooking, sewing and learning how to serve and to be polite.

To Nonyas, it was not only a matter of wealth and education but more emphasis was placed on manners.

In our houses, there were many parlours. We stayed only in the third parlour after the work was done. The first parlour was for the men, your father's friends and your brother's friends. We seldom went there. The second parlour was for our mother and our mother's friends. The parlours were separated by beautiful screens which we used to peep out of. We had beautiful fine furniture and it was the daughter-in-law's job to polish the furniture. We were trained to polish with just enough strength otherwise we would polish off all the gold finish.

During my time 50 years ago, a daughter-in-law served her mother-in-law and father-in-law hand and foot. When I first got married I got up at 6.00 a.m. every morning. I cleaned all the photographs in the house, over 200 of them, and then we prepared the betel-nut tray for my mother-in-law. Every morning flower-sellers would come and I would choose the flowers for my mother-in-law's hair. This was our education, this was our school. We had to combine the colours of the flowers so that they would look nice in our mother-in-law's hair.

When we got married, we were only 14, 15, 16 and 17 years old. We never played with dolls, played with boys or even giggled. We were not allowed to do that. If you go to Chinatown, you will see windows with louvres. When we were young, we couldn't just look out of the windows. When we wanted to see what was going on down the road, we just peeped through the louvres.

To the Nonyas, refinement was very important. We had to know how to receive guests. We had to know how to serve them. We had to know how to embroider very fine work. My mother-in-law was like a mother to me.

Our parents didn't want us to be educated because they wanted to choose our husbands for us. If we got educated we would want to choose our own husbands. Secondly, we would write love letters. Thirdly, we might disobey our parents. When I was young, I had to stand at the back of my mother-in-law and fan her while she gambled. If we had education, we would not have done this.

I can remember when it was my turn to get married, my father called me into the room and asked me to kneel down. He said to me, 'In two weeks' time you are going to get married, you are like my fingers and fingers can be dislocated. I feel as if I am removing one of my fingers. Please do not disgrace me. I have trained you for the last 10 years and you must do what you have been trained for. If you are married, your husband's mother will be your mother, his father will be your father and his sisters and brothers will be your sisters and brothers. Don't think of me and of your family at home, but you can come to see us once in a while.'

I was educated a little. But, my father was not happy about it, so eventually I had to stop.

Although our in-laws were very strict, they took very good care of us. We had to be obedient but they were responsible for us. They took care of all the things that we needed. They brought us the best of jewellery, the best dresses, the best of everything. And if there was an invitation, they would send me. Then people would say, 'Wow! look at Mrs. Lee's daughter-in-law, how well dressed she is and look at her jewellery.' When my mother-in-law died, everything went to me as her son's wife, not to her own daughter. This is the only privilege. After she died, I became the mistress of the house. It was a hard life but as I grew older and had children, I felt that they taught us well. I felt nearer to her than my own family because she scolded me, she trained but she cared for me. Later, hatred became responsibility and slowly it turned into respect. That was my experience. As she grew older, she depended more on me.

To the Nonyas, we could tell if a person was refined or not just by the way they place rice on the plate. If the rice was too little, my mother-in-law would say, 'Are you from a farmer's house? Because you are so poor that you cannot have enough rice to eat.' If we put too much rice on the plate, she would say, 'Are you a coolie? Because a coolie eats a lot of rice and little food.' So, we had to do things just right. It was difficult to be a Nonya but what really made a Nonya different was refinement.

That was her life and yet it was also perfectly in the Baba tradition that her son Lee Kuan Yew should have gone to Cambridge.

. . . *Samsui Sisters*

... *Chinese hawker*

149

The dominant Chinese culture of Singapore has enriched the lives of both Baba and emigrant Chinese. There is a fascinating contrast, however, between the emigrant Chinese culture and the old expatriate British longing for 'Home'. Many Chinese went home to China in the end, but Singapore was all theirs while they were living in it; they never despised it as second best.

From the separate sins and virtues of the old Singapore, that *riotous, volatile, unstable, unpredictable society*, in Lee Kuan Yew's words, from the protected world of his mother, and of Singapore's Indian and Malay girls in similar situations, from the English legacy, the wholeness of Singapore is emerging; though like a creature rising from the sea, it is not yet all visible. It may look like nothing else, despite the Western trappings.

It is fitting that Singapore's symbol is an animal not like any other, the merlion. The critic Kirpal Singh, in a vigorous essay on Edwin Thumboo's poem *Ulysses by the Merlion*, writes:

If Ulysses is important as a symbol, the Merlion is equally significant. Visitors to Singapore will see Singapore's Merlion at the mouth of the Singapore river, majestically spouting a spray of water from its lighted mouth into the sea. The Merlion is Singapore's emblem, combining within it the concept of a lion-city (from the original Sanskrit of which Singapore gets its name) and the importance of the sea. The Merlion, explains Thumboo, is a man-shaped symbol uniting sea and technology, with Singapore's history. The island peoples of Singapore came from the sea, the sea continues to play a vital role in the country's economy. So that the Merlion truly becomes 'this image of themselves;' it marks the transition of the non-developed island into a throbbing centre of world trade.

Thumboo's poem distils the essence of Singapore's wholeness, and the strange shape it has to take. (It is worth remarking that Thumboo is a real Singaporean, a Professor of English born of Indian and Chinese parents.)

ULYSSES BY THE MERLION

*I have sailed many waters,
Skirted islands of fire, emerged
From bouts with Circe
Who loved the squeal of pigs;
Passed Scylla and Charybdis,
Moved seven years with Calypso
Heaved in battle against the gods.
Beneath it all
I kept faith with Ithaca, travelled,
Travelled and travelled,
Suffering much, enjoying a little;
Met strange people singing
New myths; made myths myself.*

*But this lion of the sea
Salt-maned, scaly, wondrous of tail,
Touched with power, insistent
On this brief promontory . . .
Puzzles.*

*Nothing, nothing in my days
Foreshadowed this
Half-beast, half-fish,
This powerful creature of land and sea.*

*Peoples settled here,
Brought to this island
The bounty of these seas,
Built towers topless as Ilium's.*

   *They make, they serve,
   They buy, they sell.*

*Despite unequal ways
Together they mutate,
Explore the edges of harmony,
Search for a centre;
Have changed their gods,
Kept some memory of their race
In prayer, laughter, the way
Their women dress and greet.
They hold the bright, the beautiful,
Good ancestral dreams
Within new visions,
So shining, urgent,
Full of what is now.*

*Perhaps having dealt in things,
Surfeited on them,
Their spirits yearn again for images,
Adding to the dragon, phoenix,
Garuda, naga, those horses of the sun,
This lion of the sea,
This image of themselves.*

. . . *Young Singapore*

Published Jany. 1830, by John Murray, London.

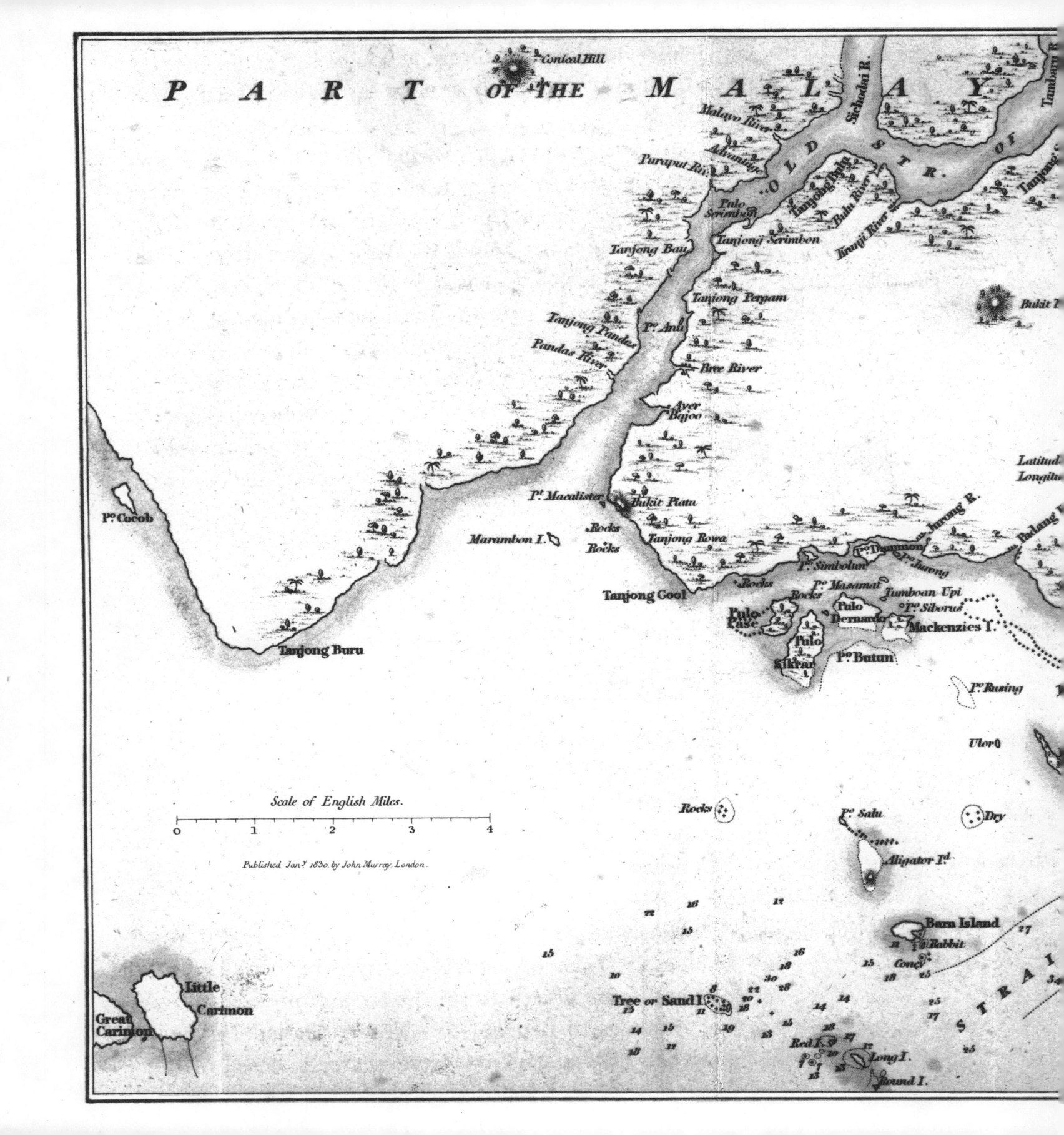